The Instant Inve

E. B. Groves was born in L   :grees of
BSc Econ. and BCom. fro   onomic
consultant specializing in c   ... include *Basic
Economic Planning Data, T*   *ne UK, Investing in the Stock
Market,* and the *Postcode Marketing Gazetteer of Britain.*

The Instant Investor

E.B. GROVES

First published in 1992
by Charles Letts & Co Ltd
Letts of London House,
Parkgate Road,
London SW11 4NQ

Copyright © E.B. Groves 1991

All our rights reserved. No part of this publication may be reproduced, stored in a retrieval system, or transmitted, in any form or by any means, electronic, mechanical, photocopying, recording or otherwise, without the prior permission in writing of the publishers.

ISBN 1 85238 190 6

A CIP catalogue record for this book is available from the British Library

'Letts' is a registered trademark of Charles Letts & Co Limited

Typeset by JCL Data Preparation, Shaftesbury, Dorset
Printed in Great Britain by Charles Letts & Co. Ltd, Dalkeith

Contents

Preface

		page
Chapter 1	**Introduction; international commercial centres; limited liability companies**	1
	International commercial centres	4
	Limited liability companies	8
Chapter 2	**The state of the art**	16
	The Big Bang	17
	London's financial markets	30
	Economic characteristics of stock markets	33
Chapter 3	**For amusement only**	36
	Personalities of the past	36
	Investor profiles of today	43
	A financial discussion	48
Chapter 4	**Aspects of risk**	51
	Investment risks of different corporate securities	53
	The investment time frame	58
	Eurotunnel	63
Chapter 5	**Stock market information and networks**	66
	Essential calculations	70
	Of shares and shareholders	76
	Capital Gains Tax	84
	Financial index numbers	85
	Economic forecasts: fact or fiction?	88
	Basic factors influencing share prices	91

v

Chapter 6	**The special situation**	99
	Recovery propositions	99
	Takeover bids	100
	Leveraged buy outs (LBOs) and management buy outs (MBOs)	107
	Arbitrage and arbitrageurs	108
	Some merits and demerits of shares in general	112
Chapter 7	**High-risk, high-return investing; crashes and crises**	114
	Traded options	114
	Traditional options	116
	Index betting	118
	Futures and options	119
	Warrants; margin trading; hedging; the short sale	121
	Business Expansion Scheme	124
	Doubtful propositions and fraudulent investments	127
	Lessons from history	129
	Speculation	138

Glossary 141

Bibliography 149

Index 152

Preface

The first-time stock market investor of the 1990s will find the dust of long-cherished market tradition only recently swept away. The introduction of major new financial legislation during the mid- and late-1980s, government privatizations and the emergence of the electronic market (Big Bang) in October 1986, have all combined to bring the activities of the International Stock Exchange (ISE), and to some extent other London financial markets, into greater prominence with the general public.

While the stock market is now, on balance, a safer place for savings, the private investor intending to play his or her own hand needs confidence, a grasp of the significance of information about shares, options and futures and a reminder that all investors can sometimes lose. Almost any punter can show a profit in a steadily rising market. A more systematic approach will usually be necessary for success in uncertain and difficult conditions.

This book is intended in part as a background introduction to investor styles past and present, and in part as a review of current information. I hope it will help inexperienced investors to avoid many obviously dangerous propositions and some of the more subtle traps for the unwary.

As London's financial markets are nothing if not fast moving, the intention has been to review current information as close as possible to publication. Every endeavour has been made to obtain information correct at 1 April 1991, including the March 1991 Budget, in so far as it affects investors.

E. B. Groves,
North Wales, 1991.

1. Introduction

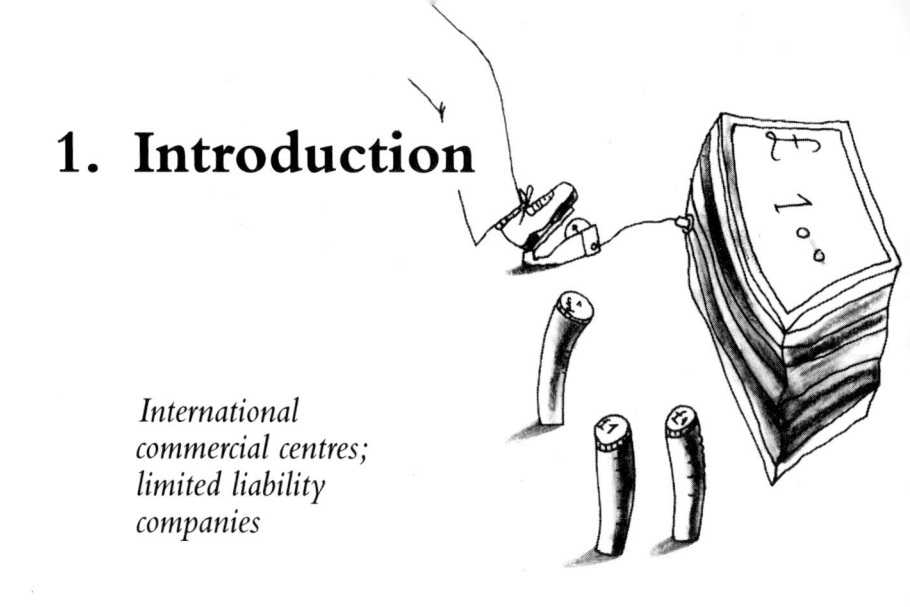

International commercial centres; limited liability companies

The dividing line separating prudent investment from wild speculation cannot be easily defined. Investments have different risk factors at different times and at different prices. The inexperienced investor needs to have his wits about him and to understand the conventions of the market in which he trades.

Investors' requirements will also vary, as will their skill and knowledge and their ability to undertake risk. What might be a normal business risk for a professional dealer in copper or rubber futures would be enormously hazardous for the private investor without experience in commodity markets. Again, some investments, such as oil exploration and gold-mining, are so inherently risky and can take so long to pay off that they can only be undertaken by the largest corporations; even then the risks are often spread by joint ventures and cross-shareholdings.

The underlying objective of investment in all its forms is to increase the value of an outlay of funds. Inherent in every investment is the express or implied intention to maximise the return on capital. The investor will operate in general within a wide legal framework, though he is not normally constrained by ethical considerations. His systematic pursuit of gain has led him to be characterised as a prime example of F. Y. Edgeworth's 'economic man' – an individual relentless in the pursuit of profit and always considering the net personal advantages of his actions. This may be an unduly harsh view of investors in general, but it goes some way to explain the competitive nature of investment where individual interests, corporate or private, are paramount.

The ethos of the 'City Man' does not embody too much loyalty to the firm or to the concept of working in a team; he is essentially an individualist. Sometimes mutual financial interests come together in a short-term venture, but the essence of the City is always competition. And while it might not be the appropriate moment, in the wake of so many recent scandals, to dwell on the business ethics embodied in some of its highest traditions (such as 'my word is my bond') the City justly regards itself as both very competitive and very professional. It expects people who transact business to know its rules and to play to them. It loves a new concept stock, adores a takeover, and quickly discards a loser.

The Barlow Clowes affair was extremely damaging to small investor confidence in the City, but unlucky or ill-advised as members of the public were in their choice of investment in this case, they were most fortunate in the generous compensation terms offered by the government.

The affairs of troubled Lloyds' syndicates have also been in and out of the headlines for the past few years. A number of investors (names) – all people of some means and from 1990 with a minimum net worth of £250,000 – now face substantial losses, and seem to have failed to grasp the full import of unlimited liability. In the case of the Outhwaite syndicate, there was a liability during 1990 of 470 per cent for investors: in other words, £470,000 for every £100,000 originally invested. This compares with the 600 per cent liability of investors in the City of Glasgow Bank, which crashed in 1878, forcing all joint stock banks to move first to a form of reserved liability and later to limited liability.

Scope of Investment

Before dealing with the scope of investment, it is important to distinguish between savings and investment. Money lodged with the Post Office, a bank or building society is correctly regarded as savings, as the nominal capital of the saver remains unchanged. The borrower – a bank, building society, or the government – assumes an obligation to pay interest, in effect the price of time, and to return the lender's capital in full on demand or in accordance with the contractual arrangements made at the outset.

Debentures of large corporations are classed as investments, as they can be traded throughout their lives and normally have a redemption date when the final holder is entitled to repayment, usually at par value. Their market prices will vary according to fluctuations in interest rates and the proximity of redemption.

Then there are ordinary shares, risk investments in the true sense. Ordinary shareholders are members of the company, not secured creditors like debenture holders. In normal circumstances ordinary shareholders can only receive repayment of capital on a capital reduction agreed by the courts under section 135 of the Companies Act 1985, or following liquidation of the company.

One of the great attractions about ordinary shares is the possibility of a capital gain which, when combined with dividends, can give a growth yield often well in excess of that available via fixed interest investment. For example, the average annual return on UK equities from 1981–7 was 21 per cent. Over the forty-four-year period 1945–89, £1000 invested in a building society would have increased at 5 per cent per year compound to yield £8557 by 1989, whereas £1000 invested in a selection of leading shares could have increased at 11 per cent per year to give a hypothetical capital sum of £98,676 in 1989.

Apart from shares and fixed-term securities such as bonds and mortgages, there are less easily traded assets like real property, leasehold interests, antiques, furniture, pictures, stamps and coins. Commodities, precious metals, traded options and futures are certainly tradeable, but they are also in the high-risk bracket and usually require expert knowledge if disappointments are to be avoided.

Thus we may safely conclude that all investments have different levels of risk, different rates of return and different time frames. A mining investment may easily have a fifteen-year payout, whereas speculation in a cargo of crude oil will give a result one way or another in a week or two.

It is sometimes said that ordinary share investors need detailed knowledge of the companies they invest in, but this is not the case. They do, however, need the ability to assess corporate financial performance and a certain skill in commercial judgement. Experienced investors always operate within their financial limits, stay within their preferred time frame, and never carry their investments to any speculative extent. The investor anticipates the impact of events, the punter reacts to them, and with all investments there is a time to buy and a time to sell. No investment is ever made for amusement only. In the market, speculative forces are always at work, and the bull and the bear prevent prices fluctuating too far from fundamental values. Investors in ordinary shares are accepting a risk in return for the expectation of dividends and a potential increase of capital value.

Ordinary shares possess two significant advantages over most other investments. They can be bought and sold at a moderate dealing cost, and the investor may make a realistic valuation of his holdings via the TV Prestel City Service or from daily newspaper closing prices on any business day of the year.

International commercial centres

The need for a mechanism and communications network for speculative purposes resulted in the establishment of organized markets and the standardization of contracts in physical commodities and financial instruments. It may be useful to note the historical explanation for the growth of particular centres, including the influences underlying the development of four towns: Antwerp, Amsterdam, London and New York, which have been successively the world's principal centres of commerce.

Antwerp

The economic law of markets suggests that where other factors are equal, trade will tend to gravitate to whichever centre offers businessmen the most advantageous balance of financial advantage.

Trade between English merchants and the Low Countries in England's staple commodity of wool had grown strongly during the fourteenth and fifteenth centuries. This activity had been assisted by ordinances since the reign of Edward I, who had also directed that trade in wool should be channelled through certain ports, to facilitate the collection of customs duties. A fourteenth-century treaty between England and Burgundy laid the foundations for further expansion of this trade. At this period Antwerp was fast becoming the centre for the warehousing and sale of wool. Antwerp, a river port some fifty-five miles from the mouth of the Scheldt, is twenty-five miles north of Brussels and about ninety miles south of Amsterdam. Its predominance was due in no small measure to its central location for distribution to the markets of northern Europe.

The discoveries of the New World in the latter part of the fifteenth century gave rise to considerable commercial expansion and, for the first time, the international movement of capital in the form of gold and silver. This reinforced Antwerp as the focus of international trade, banking and warehousing by the early sixteenth century. However, towards the end of that century a series of religious wars damaged Antwerp's commercial standing and much of its profitable commerce passed to Amsterdam and to a lesser extent to London. The final blow came following the Treaties of Westphalia in 1648, whereby the Dutch obtained the right to close the mouth of the Scheldt, with disastrous results for Antwerp.

However, it has shown a strong revival in recent years, coinciding with an improvement in the economic importance of the predominantly Dutch-speaking area of Flanders, the northern part of Belgium. By 1990, Antwerp had re-established itself as Europe's second port and one of the world's leading diamond centres.

Amsterdam

The financial community of Amsterdam was not slow to take advantage of the decline of Antwerp. In 1609 the Bank of Amsterdam was founded, at the outset mainly for the purpose of dealing in foreign exchange. During most of the seventeenth century the financial expertise made available to Dutch businessmen through the flotation of loans, development of trade credit and the existence of a stable currency, combined to give Holland a significant commercial advantage over English and other competitors in international trade. However, the establishment of the Bank of England in 1694 and the increase in international trade following the Treaty of Utrecht of 1713, which ended the War of Spanish Succession, were favourable to English commerce in general and to the importance of London as a commercial centre in particular.

The Treaty of Paris, ending the Seven Years' War in 1763, consolidated British territorial possessions in North America, India and the more important sugar-producing islands of the West Indies. In the years following 1763, we may be justified in concluding that London had drawn level with Amsterdam as one of the two leading financial centres. The importance of Amsterdam was damaged when Holland allied itself in 1795 with France in her war with Britain from 1793 to 1797. The Dutch suffered a serious reverse in 1797 at the naval battle of Camperdown, which eliminated any danger of an invasion of England by France and Holland.

London

The precise year in which London superseded Amsterdam as the world's leading commercial centre may be the subject of historical debate, but there is no doubt that Wellington's victory over Napoleon at Waterloo on 18 June 1815 laid the foundation stone for London's unrivalled commercial supremacy and cleared the way for Britain to dominate world export markets for manufactures during the remainder of the nineteenth century. In 1819 Lord Castlereagh, the British Foreign Secretary, declared the year 1818 'the most favourable year ever for British commerce'.

There were, of course, immediate financial effects of Waterloo on London and Paris as rival financial centres. In London, prices of government securities moved up strongly as the official bank rate and bond yields fell to take account of the diminished demand for money for military purposes. In Paris, as one might expect, the effect was opposite. Prices of high-yielding French *rentes* fell heavily, thus raising the yields further in line with higher general market rates, which anticipated the French government having to raise loans to finance reparations. The Second Treaty of Paris, late in 1815, confirmed the worst fears of French financiers, as it required France to pay the very substantial total of £28m in reparations to the Allies. Judging by the number of statues of the Duke of Wellington erected in towns all over England in the years after 1815, the commercially beneficial effects of his great victory were by no means lost on the British business community.

The City of London developed strongly from the 1850s, having surmounted the major financial crises and stock market panics of 1825, 1839, 1847, 1857 and 1866. The importance of London in banking, finance, shipping, insurance and as an entrepôt centre, combined with its unique location at the geographical centre of the universe – 0 degrees longitude on the Greenwich meridian – consolidated London's position. It was also the centre of government for Britain and the British empire, and by the end of the nineteenth century English was fast displacing French as the principal language of commerce.

New York

After the end of hostilities in 1918, the United States emerged as a huge creditor nation, since Britain had been forced into a heavy sale of sterling assets to pay for the war. After 1880 America had displaced Britain as the world's largest economy based on her output of crude steel. Combined with the drain of gold from London to New York, this weakened London's position further. Instead of allowing incoming gold to enter the US monetary system and expand credit, causing internal prices to rise, which would have encouraged imports to America and handicapped its export trade, resulting in an eventual return flow of bullion from the US, the United States Federal Reserve Banks effectively demonetized much of the gold inflow, which locked the automatic mechanism of the gold exchange standard. Great Britain was finally forced to relinquish the gold standard in 1931 and move to a managed currency. This further depressed London's international prestige and was a major factor in the formation of a national government in that year.

Towards the close of the Second World War in 1944, the Bretton Woods Agreement was concluded between Great Britain and the United States under which the American loan facility of £930m was granted to Britain so that she could repay the United States for its Lend-Lease assistance during 1942–5.

By the end of the 1940s the United States was again the major creditor nation of the world, with a gross national product about ten times that of the United Kingdom, though its population was only approximately four times as large. The United States rebuilt the shattered postwar economy of

Japan, dominated the World Bank for Reconstruction and Development, and by the late 1960s was accounting for around 30 per cent of world gross national product. All these factors served to underline America's enormous economic potential, with New York as the focal point for finance and the strategic centre of world politics by virtue of its having provided the home for the United Nations Assembly.

Adverse factors now affecting New York, however, include a steady decline in financial and service sector employment, such as banking and advertising, coupled with a reduction in the number of jobs in light manufacturing. Wall Street itself shed approximately 90,000 jobs during the seventeen years after the 1974 crash. High state taxes and living costs in New York City – the highest in America – must also have played their part in causing a reduction in the number of corporate headquarters in New York of *Fortune*'s Top 500 businesses: down from 128 in 1965 to 43 in 1990.

Meanwhile, during the 1950s and 1960s, London's political influence and its commercial position had been in decline. Greater London's residential population, down from 8.25m in 1951 to 6.75m by 1987 and still sliding, the development of out-of-town shopping centres, high rentals and the introduction of the uniform business rate in 1990, have all contributed to reduced trade for retail businesses in central London and a consequent decline in its status as a marketing centre.

By the end of the 1960s London docks no longer functioned to any significant extent, and much of its trade in shipping had been lost to Rotterdam – then as now the world's leading port for petroleum products and general cargo – and other continental ports. What remained of the Port of London's maritime connection was transferred twenty-five miles down river to the new container port of Tilbury. Business in freight parcels, voyage and time charters and sales of ships on the Baltic Exchange fell away with the decline in traffic in the Port of London.

Lloyds, the internationally renowned insurers, were facing intense competition in marine, aviation and general insurance, and the huge financial scandals of 1983 coupled with heavy losses resulting from Lloyds' serious misjudgement of computer obsolescence risks shook the foundations of many basic City maxims, not the least important of which was *'le mot d'un Anglais'*. The financial disasters affecting the Stock Exchange during the 1980s were no less damaging to London's commercial prestige, but it is to be hoped and is confidently expected that the stock market has entered calmer waters following the financial legislation of the mid and late 1980s. The City of London will undoubtedly survive and hopefully retain its position as the leading monetary centre of Europe in the face of increasing competition from such financial markets as Paris, Amsterdam and Frankfurt.

Finally, mention must be made of the rapid growth of Tokyo as a financial centre since 1965. Tokyo's stock market turnover is now equal to that of New York and London combined, and some of its merchant banking houses and stockbrokers are much larger in terms of capital employed than their New York or London counterparts. At present growth rates, Japan, whose revitalized economy is still in its growth phase, looks set to forge ahead of the United States of America, which is in a much later stage of economic maturity, by the end of the second decade of the twenty-first century.

Nevertheless, New York, at present first in banking and finance, with its infinite ingenuity in the creation of new speculative opportunities in a wide variety of financial instruments such as traded options, stock index options, futures, interest rate swaps, junk bonds and a whole range of leveraged investment options, makes it a tough proposition for any financial centre to challenge its supremacy in the foreseeable future.

Limited liability companies

The joint stock company has existed for centuries. The East India Company was established as a regulated company in 1600 as Lloyds of London, where members compete against each other but, according to established rules, it became joint stock in 1612. The Turkey Company, established in 1606, became joint stock in 1661. Britain is the home of both the joint stock and the limited liability company,[1] a later development of the joint stock company. From 1855 to 1862 company legislation was entered to protect the investor from unlimited losses, which had occurred with distressing regularity following the successive crises of 1825, 1839 and 1847. The panic of 1847, caused partly by intense speculation in railway shares, resulted in the suspension of the 1844 Bank Charter Act. This permitted the Bank of England to issue notes beyond the fixed limits imposed by the Act, thus guaranteeing convertibility, which quickly restored business confidence.

Nowadays the practical effect for the investor in shares or stock of a limited company (the two terms mean virtually the same, except that stock must always be fully paid) is:

1. An investor can *in no circumstances* lose more than his original investment provided the shares are fully paid.

---

[1] Though a form of limited liability existed in both the United States and France before British legislation of 1855.

2. Liability is *limited to par value or the issue price* in the case of partly paid shares.

The Companies Act 1980 defines two classes of limited liability company: public companies and private companies. The minimum number of members for a public company was reduced by this Act from seven to two. A public company must use the initials PLC (public limited company) after its name, and it may offer its shares and debentures to the public. PLCs may also be limited by guarantee, members undertaking to contribute a fixed maximum amount in the event of a liquidation. This type of company, which may not now be registered with a share capital, is frequently used by professional and trade associations and charities.

There are over half a million private companies using 'Limited' after their names, many of which are small family businesses. These companies may not invite the public to subscribe for their shares or debentures. Further, the secretary of a private company in his capacity as registrar may refuse to register any transfer of shares.

Of small technical interest are unlimited companies where, as the description suggests, members are fully liable for all its financial obligations. These are comparatively rare, but are often used in the case of large landed estates, where perpetual succession is more important than the limitation of liability. Another advantage is that, unless they are a holding or subsidiary company of another limited company, they are not required to file an annual report and accounts, thus saving considerable expense.

Company formation and meetings

The formation of public and private limited companies is similar. However, a PLC must have a minimum of £50,000 share capital, on which 1 per cent capital duty of £500 has been paid, before the Registrar of Companies will issue the necessary certificate to commence business.

Company registration agents perform the required formalities and for a fee of around £150 will effect registration and supply all the statutory books and registers. The quality of service of different registration agents varies considerably. Registered non-trading companies are available off the shelf for a slightly higher charge. A company must have, *inter alia*:

- A name
- A registered office
- Certificate of incorporation
- A memorandum of association – a summary of its principal objects

Articles of association – regulations by which its day to day administration is to be conducted
- Share register, which must be open to a shareholder's inspection free of charge and to inspection by any other person at a nominal charge
- Register of directors and secretary
- Register of charges, i.e. debentures

Any person above the age of eighteen may be a company director, though there are certain restrictions which may affect directors over seventy. A director need not necessarily be a member (shareholder) of the company, though this can be difficult at times, as a non-member director would not be able to vote.

In recent years there has been some abuse of the protection of limited liability given to company directors. A whole series of Companies Acts from 1967 to 1985 has sought to define more clearly the position of a company director. However, the most far-reaching changes are incorporated in the Insolvency Act of 1985 and the Companies Act of 1985.

Their provisions include:

1. Courts have the power to disqualify directors for a period of up to fifteen years for wrongful trading, i.e. allowing a company to trade when the directors knew or should have known it was insolvent; they may also be disqualified for misapplication of company property.

2. Penalties for failing to keep proper accounts, or for non-compliance with registration requirements, have been set at a maximum £2000 penalty for failing to file returns or accounts. The annual return within forty-two days of the Annual General Meeting (AGM); accounts within seven months of the year end for PLCs and ten months for private limited companies.

3. Directors are personally liable for debts of the company arising from wrongful trading.

In fact, most large creditors were skilful at protecting themselves before the introduction of this recent legislation. Banks lending money on debenture have taken debenture holder's action and foreclosed in certain circumstances such as non-payment of interest. An administrative receiver is then appointed to look after the creditor's (debenture holder's) interests and run the company to ensure a full recovery of the loan and interest wherever possible. Again, banks effectively neutralize limited liability protection by obtaining personal guarantees for loans to the company from directors of smaller private companies. Legally this means the directors have pledged repayment of the company's bank borrowing to the full extent of their personal wealth, often an extremely high-risk and open-ended commitment.

These guarantees give the banker a dual strategy in the event of financial difficulty or cash flow problems causing the borrower to exceed agreed limits for an extended period. Business development loans will usually have been secured by a fixed charge (first mortgage) on freehold land or buildings, or if this is not possible by a floating charge over all the company's assets. In the case of a fixed charge, the bank is usually content to rely on its security. A holder of a floating charge also has the legal right to appoint an administrative receiver, as mentioned earlier.

Reinforced by personal guarantees, the bank often finds it cheaper and more effective to insist on repayment of the guaranteed overdraft or other borrowing by the guarantors as a first course of action. Here the position of joint guarantors may be of interest, as illustrated by a case history: Three people decided to register a limited company with the object of acting as marketing consultants, each giving his own personal guarantee of the firm's overdraft, thus overriding limited liability. Several years later one of the directors decided to leave. As the overdraft was still running, the bank considered their security weakened by his withdrawal, and asked him for a substantial payment to release him from his obligation under the guarantee.

The legal significance of these guarantees has caused a great deal of trouble in the last few years, with large numbers of inexperienced people setting themselves up as self-employed.[2] Frequently, the signatory to a guarantee does not understand the serious consequences of a default or indeed what he or she is guaranteeing. So much so that at least one high-street bank now sends the forms to its customer's solicitor before completing any financial arrangements.

Public utilities such as gas, electricity and the telephone service will ask for deposits where they notice directors of companies which went into liquidation trading again as new limited liability companies. And, of course, the Inland Revenue, Customs and Excise and rating authorities all rank as preferential creditors in the event of a collapse.

Large suppliers are also well aware of their legal rights to stop goods in transit (stoppage *in transitu*) if news of a buyer's insolvency reaches them. In many instances terms of sale have been altered so that the property in the goods does not pass to the buyer until payment is made. This prevents the liquidator seizing goods already delivered but not paid for, and leaving the

---

[2] Numbers of self-employed are up from 2.2m in June 1983 to 3.4m in June 1990.

trade supplier with only the unsecured creditor's right to prove his claim in a winding-up, with the probability of recovering no more than a fraction of his claim.

Thus it follows that smaller trade creditors and members of the public are the least protected, because they do not know what courses of action are open to them and find it difficult to obtain information on the company's current financial position.[3] Even after the latest legislation has been enacted, limited liability is still providing a useful shield for many company directors and some protection for investors.

Every company must hold an *Annual General Meeting* (AGM) in each calendar year. Not more than fifteen months must elapse between meetings, except that the first AGM may be held any time up to eighteen months from date of incorporation. Normally, directors will convene the meeting and must give twenty-one days' notice to members. The annual report and accounts are forwarded to shareholders in time for the AGM. Anyone else can obtain the report and accounts by requesting a copy from the company secretary. Many AGMs are in practice little more than meetings to obtain the shareholders' approval of the accounts and dividend and the reappointment of auditors.

An *Extraordinary General Meeting* may be convened by directors at any time or, subject to the articles, by two or more members holding 10 per cent of the issued capital.

An *Ordinary Resolution* must be passed by a simple majority exceeding 50 per cent of those present, voting by show of hands.

Extraordinary and Special Resolutions must be passed by a 75 per cent majority of those present and voting.

Any five members or members representing 10 per cent of the voting rights or 10 per cent of the issued capital may *demand a poll* – a full count of votes represented by the shareholders present plus proxies lodged – with each share normally carrying one vote. Preference shares may carry the same voting rights as ordinary shares, but this is not usual unless there are dividend arrears.

---

[3] Fees for searches at Companies House, London EC1, Cardiff and Edinburgh as at 1 January 1990

1.1 Standard search (availability one hour): £2.50 per company
1.2 Premium search (availability twenty minutes): £20.00 per company
　　　　　　　　　Photocopies: 10p per sheet
　　　　　　　　　Computer screen print: 50p
2. Postal service: (normally three-day service): £4 per company
　 Photocopy service: £5.50 per company
3. Fax service (sixty-minute turn round): £30 minimum plus £1 per page above fifteen pages.

A *proxy* is any person appointed by a member to vote on his or her behalf at a company meeting. The proxy need not be a shareholder. In practice, a shareholder agreeing with a proposal will, if not attending, appoint the chairman as his proxy by returning the voting card. Postal votes must normally be returned at least forty-eight hours before any company meeting to allow the secretariat time for collation.

Auditors are independent firms of chartered or certified accountants appointed to protect shareholders. They verify the accuracy of the company's accounts, which must be presented in a form to give 'a true and fair view' of the company's financial position at the date of compilation. Auditors may qualify the accounts if in their opinion they do not meet the requirements of the Companies Acts. They are appointed by the directors but can only be removed by a resolution of members at an AGM: Companies Act 1985, S.386. Company auditors also have the right to attend AGMs even though they are neither shareholders nor employees: *ibid.*, section 387, and they are usually appointed scrutineers on a poll.

Administrators and liquidation

The Insolvency Act 1985 introduced a new class of financial manager for a company in difficulty.

Under section 28 a company, its directors or any creditor may petition the court for an administration order under which an administrator is appointed. The order cannot be granted where a company is already in receivership or liquidation, with the proviso that if the person or organization appointing the receiver agrees, an administration order can supersede receivership. The holder of a floating charge may do this to save expense, provided he is satisfied that his position under an administrator, who may not be his nominee, will in no way be weakened.

Section 30 gives a company under administration very powerful protection during the existence of the order. For example, no receiver may be appointed, no winding-up order made, nor resolution to wind up passed, no execution nor enforcement of judgement against the company is permitted, nor may legal proceedings against the company be commenced or continued. In effect, this is similar to Chapter 11 of the United States Bankruptcy Laws, as the administration order gives the company a breathing space by virtue of the standstill on all legal claims and creditors' moves.

Section 27 states, *inter alia*, that the court will grant an administration order to assist the survival of a company, in whole or in part, or where the order would result in a more advantageous realization of assets than would be effected on a winding-up.

From the beginning of 1987 until the end of 1990, of 129 companies which appointed administrators, only ten returned to solvency. Of those that failed the creditors received an average of 12p in the £.

As has been shown, starting a company, like getting married, can be a relatively inexpensive procedure. Company liquidation, like divorce, is decidedly expensive, though a most unlikely occurrence in the case of listed companies.

The share quotation is normally suspended on the appointment of a liquidator. However, even a non-trading listed company without tangible assets possesses a value as a 'shell', providing a vehicle for a non-listed company to obtain at a later stage a cheap stock market listing. Its tax losses, if any, are, in certain circumstances, a negotiable asset, transferable to the purchasing company.

The alternative ways in which a company may be wound up are:

1. By the court under section 517 of the Companies Act 1985. This is termed compulsory liquidation, with the Official Receiver normally acting as liquidator.

2. A members' voluntary liquidation under section 579. In this case the directors make a declaration of solvency to the effect that all debts will be paid in full.

3. A creditors' voluntary liquidation under section 587. The procedure is similar to the members' voluntary liquidation, but there is no declaration of solvency. The liquidator is appointed at the first meeting of creditors, usually by the principal creditor.

In theory, any creditor whose debt of more than £750 has not been satisfied within twenty-one days of notice being served at the company's registered office, may petition the court for a compulsory liquidation. In practice this will be expensive as company liquidation proceedings take place in the High Court in the case of companies whose issued capital exceeds £120,000. Additionally, where a company's assets appear unlikely to cover the Official Receiver's expenses, the petitioner will usually be required to lodge a minimum of £3000 deposit as a contribution to the expenses of liquidation.

The essence of liquidation is that the company's assets are reduced to cash. Creditors are paid in full, having regard to the priority claims of preferential creditors and debenture holders. The liquidator has a prior claim for his own administrative expenses, which often represent a very substantial proportion of net realized assets in the case of small and medium-sized concerns. Any surplus remaining is then available for the preference and ordinary shareholders.

Obviously, a less expensive alternative would be welcome. This is only possible in very exceptional circumstances. Under section 652 of the Companies Act 1985, a defunct, non-trading company without assets or liabilities may be removed from the register by a simple exchange of correspondence between the company secretary, the directors and the company. After formal notification, the registrar will strike off the company. The object here is to save the cost of making annual returns, directors' reports and accounts. Dormant companies are spared the cost of appointing auditors by section 252 of the Companies Act 1985.

An alternative to liquidation is the company reconstruction scheme often dictated by debenture holders, usually banks. On the subject of reconstruction it is interesting to note that the purchase of shares by American companies as a takeover defence has sometimes brought about an effective capital reconstruction. This device is, of course, now available to UK companies under section 162 of the 1985 Companies Act and was permitted by the 1981 Companies Act. It is, however, an extremely expensive and limited option which can result in a very high-geared structure, unsuitable for many companies. Most reconstruction arrangements will protect the interests of the secured creditors and often increase the risk for ordinary shareholders. What individual shareholders do in such circumstances will be a matter of judgement based on their view of the prospects for recovery, supplemented by expert professional advice where a complex arrangement is proposed, the extent of their financial involvement, and the capital losses they may have already suffered.

2. The State of the Art

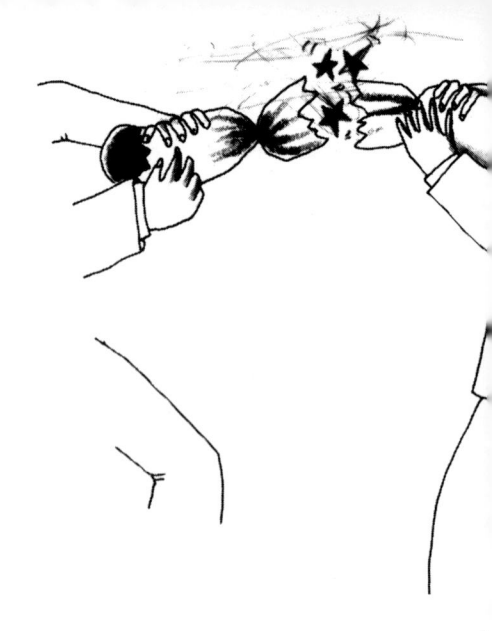

Before considering the fundamental changes caused by the Big Bang it may be useful to recall how the system of share dealing worked in former days. The underlying principles were:

(i) single capacity trading, that is to say jobbers or market makers were independent of stockbrokers, who acted as agents of the investor. The jobber had no direct contact with the investing public;

(ii) when obtaining a price for dealing, the broker did not disclose his position to the jobber. In this way, by not giving an indication of whether he was a buyer or a seller, the jobber's price was not influenced.

To illustrate the practical working of the former system, suppose Mr Jones, a client of ABC Brokers, was interested in buying 5000 Tarmac ordinary shares at best. Having received the client's instruction, a representative of ABC would approach jobbers known to deal in Tarmac. On finding the best price, say 278 (bid)/282 (offered), he would place the order to buy 5000 Tarmac ordinary at 282p, advising Mr Jones of the price that day. A contract note would be issued by the broker, and the client would acquire all rights in the shares on the issue of this document. (For an example of contract notes, see Chapter Five.) Settlement would be ten days after the close of the current Stock Exchange trading account, which normally runs for two weeks.

The Big Bang

One of the principal changes brought in by the Big Bang of 27 October 1986 was that the old single capacity system of stock and share trading changed. Many brokers combined with jobbers to fulfil the dual function of broker and jobber (market maker). Additional finance poured into the restructured stockbrokers, now facing intense competition from large American and Japanese brokerage houses which had established themselves in London. There remain, however, a number of brokers who are not market makers.

The Big Bang might, to the casual observer, have carried the implication that all four aspects of share trading – quotation, dealing, settlement and registration – were computerized from that date. In fact, TALISMAN, the computer settlement system, was introduced in 1978. TOPIC, the database, had been available in a restricted form since 1980. SAEF, the automatic execution in rotation facility for 1000 share orders or less, was expected to be operational during 1992. Only SEAQ, electronic price quotations and an expansion of TOPIC, came onstream on 27 October 1986. Nevertheless, the electronic revolution undoubtedly ushered in a new era. Many, but not all, stock market investors obtained cheaper investment as a result of the Big Bang, in addition to safer investment following consolidation of company law and the introduction of new protective legislation.

By the end of 1990 some 800 employees out of the ISE workforce of 3200 had been made redundant or retired; 100 standing committees and special interest groups had been reduced to just four, accounting systems had been streamlined, and company registrars invited on to the board of the Settlement Services Division. ISE investigation teams now prosecute all insider dealing cases, and a regulatory news service started announcements on 3 December 1990.

Computerized share trading systems

The Stock Exchange Clearing House was established in 1873. The computerized share settlement system, TALISMAN, has been in operation for some thirteen years. The basis for the system is the establishment of a nominee account in the register of all participating companies: SEPON (Stock Exchange pool nominees), and all purchases and sales are transferred to SEPON. Computerized settlement is effected between brokers and the centre on account day.

The rolling four-day settlement system, similar to that in use on Wall Street, will replace the existing fortnightly account system some time in

17

1992. Under the new system the investor buying or selling shares on a Monday will settle on the following Friday. Tuesday deals will be for settlement the following Monday, four business days later, and so on. Thus under the new system the investor will deal on Day 1 and pay on Day 5, compared with the present system where an investor may deal on any of the ten trading days of the account, settling six business days after the account closes.

The ISE expects to privatize its settlement service during 1992 in time for the introduction of TAURUS (transfer and registration of uncertificated stocks). It will retain ownership of the TALISMAN and TAURUS systems, providing the electronic settlement service under contract to the new Clearing House. The ISE is to have a 60 per cent stake in the Clearing House with banks, financial institutions and insurance companies being offered a share of the remaining 40 per cent. The introduction of TAURUS will result in a loss of around 3000 Stock Exchange jobs by 1994.

The existing system of share registration, dating back to 1844, involves the issue of a share certificate as documentary evidence that a shareholder's name and address have been entered in the register. An example of a certificate for 6000 shares is shown below (Figure 1, reproduced by kind permission of Lonrho PLC, London).

No. of Certificate	Transfer No.(s)	Date	Number of Shares
294851	39921	18 APR 79	---6,000---

ORDINARY SHARES

LONRHO LIMITED

(Incorporated under the Companies (Consolidation) Act, 1908.)
(now LONRHO PLC under Companies Act, 1980)

THIS IS TO CERTIFY that

is/are the Registered Holder(s) of **SIX THOUSAND ***
ORDINARY SHARES of twenty-five pence each, fully paid, in the above-named Company subject to the Memorandum and Articles of Association of the Company.

GIVEN under the Common Seal of the Company on the date written above

NOTE: No transfer of shares comprised in this Certificate, or any portion thereof, will be registered until this Certificate has been surrendered.
Registrars: National Westminster Bank Limited, Registrar's Department, P.O. Box 82, National Westminster Court, 37 Broad Street, Bristol BS99 7NH.

CE/620/A/--

Figure 1, Share Certificate

Loss of a share certificate causes problems and can be expensive. Banks charge up to £20 for signing a letter of indemnity to protect the registrar from loss arising from the issue of a replacement certificate when the original may still be in existence. Instead of a fixed fee, banks sometimes charge 0.25 per cent of the value of the shares, which can represent a substantial cost to the shareholder. An example of a letter of indemnity is included for purposes of illustration (Figure 2).

Although some medium-sized listed companies maintain their own share register under the control of the company secretary, the most common practice today is for a high-street bank or other professional registrar to be appointed. Lloyds Bank and NatWest control about 65 per cent of the share registration market, with Barclays (having recently purchased Hill Samuel Registrars), Midland and the non-bank registrars such as Ravensbourne Securities and Regis sharing the remainder.

All large share registers are now computerized. Figure 3, an extract from a computerized register, shows the entries in a shareholder's account in respect of purchases, sales, rights and scrip issues over a ten-year period.

To complement TALISMAN, TAURUS is being introduced in April 1993, with completion by the end of 1993.[1] Stockbrokers and banks are to be designated direct account holders: TACS, within the TAURUS system. Shareholders' names and addresses will be stored in the system, with TACS maintaining sub-registers instead of a single registrar maintaining a complete share register, as at present. Direct account holders may effect computer enquiries about their own holdings and will send details of holdings to shareholders from time to time. Dividends will continue to be paid in the usual way; settlement of share transactions will be speeded up, and share certificates eliminated, although shareholders will still receive contract notes. Those who wish to have share certificates will remain outside the system, with the registration and issue of certificates by registrars continuing as at present. Without the vital share certificate, the possibilities of computer fraud and the difficulty for a shareholder in the TAURUS system of establishing a claim to a shareholding the computer erroneously says he has sold, are likely to present the system's designers and shareholders of the future with certain problems.

---

[1] In March 1990 the ISE announced: the introduction of a four-day rolling settlement system by October 1992; that paperless settlement will come into effect by December 1993. Individual companies will vote to join the scheme using a block voting system based on the numbers of shares held. Maximum claim for an individual shareholder will be £250,000. DTI has regulatory control, with ISE in charge of day to day operational control.

9 September 1987

LETTER OF INDEMNITY

To: The Directors,

The original Certificate(s) of title relating to the undermentioned Stock/Shares of the above-named Company ("the Company") has/have been lost or destroyed.

Neither the Stock/Shares nor the Certificate(s) of title thereto has/have been transferred, charged, lent or deposited or dealt with in any manner affecting the absolute title thereto of the person(s) named in the said Certificate(s) and such person(s) is/are entitled to be on the Register in respect of such Stock/Shares.

We, the undersigned, hereby jointly and severally agree in consideration of your issuing in the name(s) of the person(s) named in the Schedule below a new Certificate(s) for the undermentioned Stock/Shares, to indemnify you and the Company from and against all actions, losses, costs, charges, claims and demands of any and every kind which may be incurred by you and/or the Company in consequence of such action on your part.

I/We undertake to deliver to the Company for cancellation the said original Certificate(s) should the same ever be recovered.

THE SCHEDULE
Particulars of Certificate(s) lost or destroyed

Certificate Number(s)	Class of Stock/Shares	Number of Shares/Stock Units	In the Name(s) of
C008465	Ordinary Shares of 5p each	2,000	

Dated this ....day of ....19 ....

Signed by**
in the Presence of

Witness's { Signature, Address, Occupation, } ....

Signed by**
in the Presence of

Witness's { Signature, Address, Occupation, } ....

Signed by***
in the Presence of

Witness's { Signature, Address, Occupation, } ....

The holder's signature(s) must be witnessed.

**Name of Stockholder/Shareholder or Agent.
***Name and status of signatory signing on behalf of a Bank, Insurance Company or Guarantee Company, which should also be named and who should impress their rubber stamp hereon.

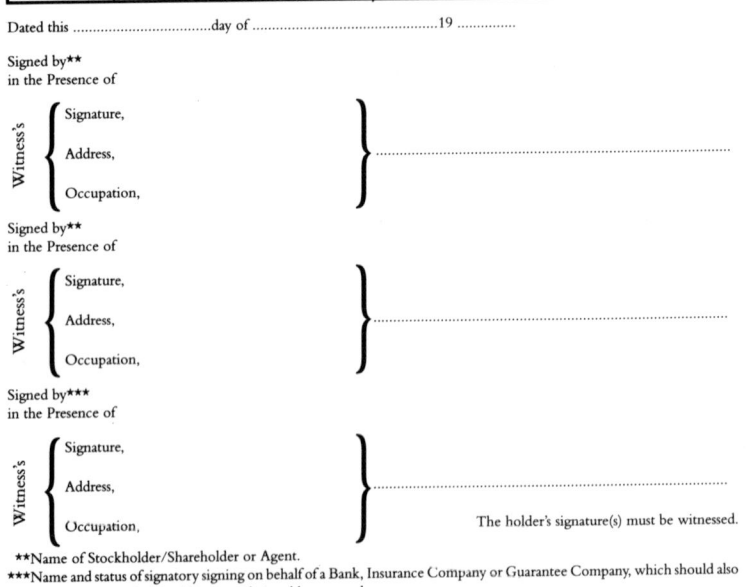

Figure 2, Sample letter of indemnity

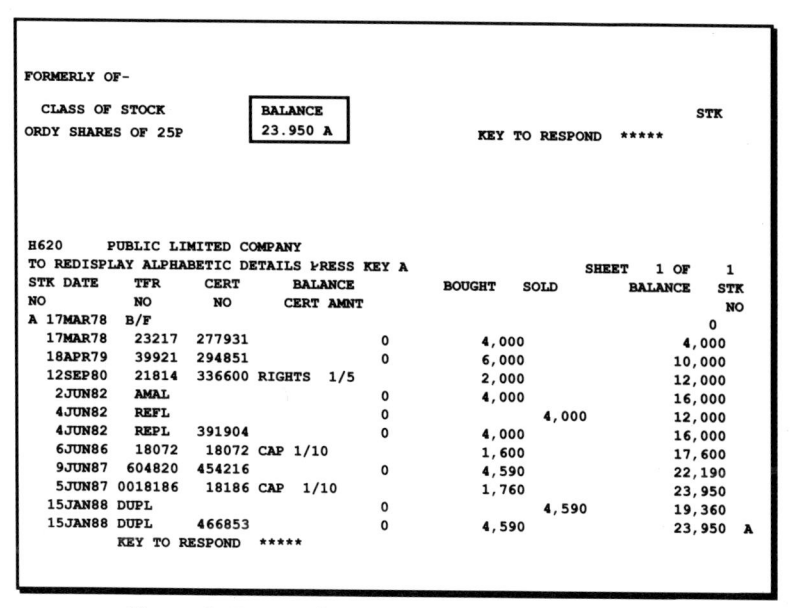

```
FORMERLY OF-
    CLASS OF STOCK                                                          STK
    ORDY SHARES OF 25P       BALANCE
                             23.950 A              KEY TO RESPOND  *****


    H620      PUBLIC LIMITED COMPANY
    TO REDISPLAY ALPHABETIC DETAILS PRESS KEY A                SHEET  1 OF  1
    STK DATE    TFR       CERT     BALANCE      BOUGHT    SOLD      BALANCE    STK
    NO          NO        NO       CERT AMNT                                   NO
    A 17MAR78   B/F                                                       0
      17MAR78   23217     277931              0    4,000                  4,000
      18APR79   39921     294851              0    6,000                 10,000
      12SEP80   21814     336600 RIGHTS 1/5        2,000                 12,000
      2JUN82    AMAL                         0    4,000                 16,000
      4JUN82    REFL                         0             4,000        12,000
      4JUN82    REPL      391904             0    4,000                 16,000
      6JUN86    18072     18072 CAP 1/10          1,600                 17,600
      9JUN87    604820    454216             0    4,590                 22,190
      5JUN87    0018186   18186 CAP 1/10          1,760                 23,950
      15JAN88   DUPL                         0             4,590        19,360
      15JAN88   DUPL      466853             0    4,590                 23,950  A
                KEY TO RESPOND     *****
```

Figure 3, Extract from computerized share register

Stock Exchange automated quotation system (SEAQ) is the real time on-line price quotation and transaction system. The system works by market makers logging on with their opening prices at the start of each trading day. Once prices are logged on, brokers may call up securities in which they are interested. Visual display units (VDUs) in brokers' offices will then indicate latest floor prices of shares and gilts. Table 1 shows the present share classification for trading purposes.

TOPIC is the supporting database of the quotations service SEAQ, and makes available comprehensive statistical information on:

- Company news and price trends
- Extel earnings projections for 500 major stocks
- Tokyo stock prices
- New York, via QUOTRON for Wall Street prices and NASDAQ for over the counter (OTC) prices
- European stock market prices
- LIFFE data on financial futures
- Traded option prices
- FOREX information
- London and New York ADR[2] prices in dollars

[2] American Depository Receipts (see glossary).

Table 1, Stock Exchange automated share classification for trading purposes

Share Category	Approximate number of companies at 31.12.90	Minimum number of market makers	ON SCREEN information available
Alpha – most active major stocks	164	10	Firm bid and asking prices. Cumulative total of trading volumes
Beta – frequently traded stocks	632	4	Firm bid and offer prices
Gamma – less active stocks	1700	2	Middle prices only
Delta – infrequently traded stocks	413	1	Matched bargains. Price indication of last transaction

Notes

1. All prices displayed are for minimum trades of 1000 shares.
2. Most unlisted securities market (USM) shares fall into Gamma or Delta classifications.
3. Average number of Alpha stock market makers = 25.
4. Touch price = Highest bid, lowest asking price.
5. The Elwes Committee of the ISE which reported in March 1990 made these recommendations:

    a) Market makers have no obligation to deal and may delay twenty-four hours before reporting trades of 100,000+ shares.

    b) Brokers must declare matching trades outside the touch range – marked PT on contract notes.

    c) The existing share classification is to be replaced by a system based on the tradeability, liquidity and volatility of each stock.

    d) That overseas members be allowed to join the ISE to maintain London's competitiveness with other stock markets in the European time zone, such as Paris and Frankfurt.

There are approximately 9000 subscribers to TOPIC, 3000 of whom subscribe to the more comprehensive level II service. Level I shows the best bid and offer quotations for alpha and beta securities for about 600 stocks; level II shows the best bid and offer prices for leading equities from registered market makers (see table).

Large investors such as banks and discount houses and other corporate investors continue to deal direct with the market makers via AERIAL – a computerized transaction-only dealing service.

SEAQ service for 2700 gilts and equities is now available to the private investor via Prestel City Service.

Other financial support systems include:

Datastream: A database of investment statistics and graphics.

Finstat: UK equities database; McCarthy ON-LINE – a full text database of financial publications.

ICC: Includes SHAREWATCH on line data of shareholders with holdings of 0.25+ per cent in UK quoted companies.

QUOTRON: Electronic quotations of stocks, options, futures and commodities.

Telerate: Foreign exchange, interest rates, Eurobond prices, precious metals.

UNICOM: Prices of commodities, options and futures supported by graphics; mathematical analysis.

It is believed that special computer tabulations are now available of certain nominee holdings by beneficial owner, and of aggregate shareholdings by company by investor.

Unlisted securities market (USM)

This second-level electronic market administered by the Stock Exchange has been in operation since 1981. It absorbed the third market after the close of the account on 28 December 1990, and at that date consisted of 413 stocks not satisfying the requirements for a full listing on the ISE. The total of 413 companies included twelve stocks listed on the former third ma.ket. Shares of the twenty-two companies not wishing to transfer to USM will henceforth be traded on a matched bargain basis under rule 535(2) (see Chapter Five for note on special trades).

The requirements for a USM listing have been eased from the date of its reconstitution with the third market, to require the submission of just two years' accounts, instead of three years' accounts, as previously. The speculative risk in such shares is thus considerably increased.

Effects of computerized procedures

The new electronic trading system has advantaged investors by narrowing the spread between bid and offer prices for major stocks. Time stamping of transactions and the surveillance of deals carrying the hallmark of irregularity provide additional safeguards, not available under the previous system. However, anxiety must still exist about certain aspects of trading. In the case of many delta stocks – infrequently traded shares – there is only one market maker. Investors with experience of the former over the counter (OTC) market in Britain will know to their cost how expensive it can be when they are sellers of shares and there is only one buyer. Introduction of an anti-monopoly regulation requiring at least two independent market makers for all delta stocks would be beneficial and reassuring to all investors.[3]

On the question of conflict of interest, it is perhaps in the advisory area that such conflict may more easily arise. Let us suppose that a substantial investor sought the advice of his broker on the merits of a purchase of 100,000 Lonrho v. 100,000 Norcross. Assume also that the broker's firm was a market maker in Norcross, was long in the stock, but did not deal in Lonrho. In such circumstances it might be thought difficult for the broker to give his client an absolutely impartial evaluation of the two alternative investments, as he would have been able to do under the previous single capacity system.

Another significant effect of Big Bang has been a substantial reduction in dealing costs[4] primarily for the larger private (middle) investor. The pre-Big Bang scale was 1.65 per cent up to £7000, 0.55 per cent from £7000–£130,000, with VAT at 15 per cent on commission; stamp duty 1 per cent on the value of the transaction. From 27 October 1986 stamp duty was reduced to 0.5 per cent, eliminated completely on the introduction of TAURUS in April 1993 and the fixed commission structure abandoned,

---

[3] In January 1991 the ISE introduced proposals to ensure at least two market makers for every share listed on the main market and for all USM stocks.
[4] The reclassification of stockbrokers from taxable to exempt VAT category with effect from 1 January 1990 has increased many brokers' commissions. Although brokerage is no longer subject to VAT on the contract note, stockbrokers are now unable to reclaim VAT input on telephone, petrol, maintenance, etc., which raises their base costs.

although some brokers tried to maintain the former rates. One north-country broker even intended to index the pre-Big Bang scale rates for inflation.

However, by the end of 1990 a typical brokerage charge was 1.65 per cent to £7000, plus 0.4 per cent above. Banks, who normally handle stock market transactions for current account customers only, had moved to an average of 1.55 per cent, with a minimum of around £20, being more used to handling transactions of low average value than many stockbrokers. The minimum charge made by brokers was also around £20–£25 for the full service, though some brokers operated a minimum of £25 for their transaction-only service. The lowest cost transaction-only services were (a) 1 per cent to a maximum of £77; (b) 1 per cent to a maximum of £100; and (c) £50 full rate fee to a maximum transaction of £20,000, plus a once-for-all charge of £25 to open an account.

This last comes with the unattractive arrangement of the broker holding clients' shares in a nominee account, and allocating dividends, which makes one wonder why it can be so wrong to hold the share certificates in your safe at home or at your bank.

VAT on share transactions was discontinued with effect from 1 January 1990. Taking the 1 per cent/£100 maximum as typical, allowing for the 0.5 per cent reduction in stamp duty, dealing expenses are approximately one-third lower at the £10,000 level of transaction and 60 per cent lower at the £50,000 level than pre-Big Bang. Share deals of £1500 and below almost certainly cost more than before Big Bang. The advantage of new commission scales should, however, start to be apparent at the £7000 level, which most brokers would consider a realistic minimum size of order to allow full overhead recovery.

The reductions in dealing costs for transaction-only clients do not include the benefit of narrower price quotations for major stocks. However, it should be recognized that the transaction-only service is, in general, for experienced investors. Yet another variation for the 'transaction only' investor is the broker's requirement that the investor open a high interest account with the broker with a minimum balance of £2500 on which interest is payable on balances above £1000. In effect, a type of account current widely used in the US for margin traders and other regular investors. Whether such an arrangement will appeal to the investor must be a matter of judgement.

Using the transaction-only service, clearing a double taxation relief query on Malay registered plantation shares necessitated telephoning a regional office of the Inland Revenue. Chasing up an overdue dividend on an *ex div* (see glossary) sale of an engineering share necessitated contacting the company's share registration department at Sheffield. Verification that a series of purchases of an oil exploration stock made in June all qualified for the July scrip dividend announced during June, required a telephone call to the Stock Exchange Official List in London as 'this information hasn't appeared on the screen'. Somehow, the broker never seems to follow through in quite the same way for transaction-only clients. There is also the point that many investors have suffered delays in settlement, where the broker adheres strictly to the rule book and settles on registration. Of course, brokers also suffer from late-paying clients. US brokers charge daily interest on all overdue balances.

In fairness to banks, they are, in general, exceptionally good in following up awkward and time-consuming queries. There is also the point that if an investor should be in dispute with a broker, a bank as agent can be no bad thing. Thus, when choosing between one broker or another, or one bank or another, experienced investors know it is not possible to determine where their balance of advantage lies simply by comparing different rates of commission.

Turning to the longer-term effects, the international computer link between London, New York, Tokyo and key European exchanges has widened the market for major British stocks. As London PE multiples (see glossary) are no more than 25 per cent of Tokyo ratings, though similar to Wall Street, this should encourage a flow of Japanese investment into London equities. It may also be interesting to note an approximation of the relative growth of market capitalizations of the world's three principal stock markets over the past forty years:

	1949	19 December 1990	
		Index	PE
London	100	1250	11
New York	100	2000	14
Tokyo	100	25000	45

A number of leading British stocks – such as Glaxo, Hanson, ICI, Bass – have been traded in ADR form on Wall Street for some time. This form of trading has now been taken up by the London market since August 1987, when forty leading stocks were first traded as ADRs.

On Wall Street, one ADR represents one or more shares, and UK dividends are grossed up for basic rate UK tax and then subject to a 15 per cent withholding tax. This withholding tax is normally allowed as a credit against federal taxes for resident US investors. The 1.5 per cent special tax in the 1986 Budget on ADRs, initiated in London, is levied on the value of shares originally converted and not on subsequent trades. Wall Street's four-day settlement procedure for delivery of and payment for securities applies to London ADRs. At some stage, international share settlement timing will be harmonized between the principal markets and facilitated by international computer transfer.

Heavy capital investment in computerization and lower average commission per deal as a result of increased competition has certainly brought about staff reductions. Payroll representing around 70 per cent of total costs and high computer expense must ultimately cause a fall in profitability in the number of stockbroking firms, unless average commission charges and turnover can be increased. To offset lower commissions, brokers must generate a corresponding increase in trading volume. Certain private investors may therefore be encouraged to increase their annual rate of capital turnover in line with the US private investor, or to move into traded options, stock index options and futures. By the end of 1990, the number of market makers in shares was down to twenty-seven and expected to go lower in the medium term.

At the institutional level, competitive commission rates are vital. In January 1991 it was estimated that the aggregate minimum daily breakeven transaction level for all stockbroking firms constituting the London market was around 500m shares traded. It also seems likely that more intensive fundamental and technical analysis will have to be undertaken by certain London brokers to retain the business of demanding institutional clients, already bypassing brokers and dealing direct with market makers for many large and uncomplicated transactions.

American and Japanese brokerage houses, newly established in London, have in general a wider-ranging and more detailed analytical research facility than their British counterparts. For example, it is by no means unique for a single Wall Street analyst to specialize in a maximum of a dozen stocks in a particular sector.

Finally, in the months immediately following Big Bang it was noticeable that day-to-day fluctuations in the FT-SE 100 Index were sharper. This may indicate an extension of speculative trading in either the cash or futures market, computerized programme trades, or possibly that the greater volatility of the New York and Tokyo markets is affecting London.

Share transactions above £5000 carry a levy of £2 from April 1991, to cover the cost of investor protection. The public might feel more confident, and marginal advisers rather less so, if investment advisers of less than five years' standing were required to establish their credentials and trade without the protection of limited liability for a period of, say, three to five years.

Sections 12–16 of Schedule I of the Financial Services Act, 1986 classify investment business as follows:

1. Managing investments for another person
2. Arranging to buy or sell for another person
3. Giving or offering advice on investments
4. Dealing in investments

It is interesting to note that newspapers, journals, magazines and presumably stock market letters, whose main purpose is not the recommendation of any specific investment, appear to be exempt from authorization by virtue of section 25 of Schedule I of the Act. An important legal distinction seems to have been made between information of a general financial nature, for which no licence is required, and investment advice directed towards a specific investment where the seller has a financial interest, which does require a licence.

Development of new regulatory authorities

The Financial Services Act of 1986 came into full effect in January 1988. It established a network of regulatory authorities supervising the whole field of investment and investor protection.

Both Lloyds and the International Stock Exchange (ISE) have been allowed to continue the administration of their own private arrangements. With particular reference to Lloyds, the public in general and investors in certain Lloyds syndicates may feel that the present system of regulation is still not up to standard.

The ISE has also been rocked in recent years by a series of financial crashes involving heavy losses to thousands of investors. The names of M. L. Doxford, Norton Warburg, Slater Walker, Connaught Latham, British & Commonwealth and Polly Peck, to say nothing of the Guinness insider scandal, come readily to mind. Plainly, some high-grade public relations work remains to be done if credibility and investor confidence are to be completely restored in both these institutions.

In the area of takeovers and mergers, the ISE authorities have moved to strengthen the administrative framework. The takeover panel's directorate now incorporates increased legal representation, although the essence of the takeover code has always been that it did not seek to rely on the force of law but on its own authority to ensure observation of its rulings. It functions principally to harmonize the interests of shareholders involved in takeover or merger situations and now has power to revoke licences of merchant banks or stockbrokers, where serious infringements of the code are shown to have occurred. Another recent innovation is the establishment of the panel's audit committee to verify that all financial transactions in a takeover have been conducted in accordance with the code.

The Securities and Investment Board (SIB) is the central co-ordinating authority for the work of self-regulatory organizations (SROs) (see chart for relationship between SIBs and other regulatory authorities and exchanges). If, for example, a Financial Intermediaries and Brokers Regulatory Association (FIMBRA) member failed and FIMBRA was unable to meet claims, investors would presumably look to the SIB as, in effect, the guarantor of the new compensation provisions.

All investment firms have needed a Department of Trade licence since November 1986. The SRO most likely to be encountered by private investors is FIMBRA (see chart).[5] Annual licence fees for members were set in 1987 at £900 per year for a typical firm, rising to £18,000 per year for a firm with 100 dealers. Maximum compensation limits for investors have been set at £48,000 – 100 per cent of the first £30,000 of loss, plus 90 per cent of the next £20,000, where the loss has arisen from the financial collapse of a FIMBRA member. The ISE is now considering reviving its former compensation scheme, which covered investors to £250,000 in the event of a stockbroker's failure. There is certainly no cover for investment losses unless, presumably, the client could show that he acted entirely on the agent's advice, which was given without due care and consideration, when the possibility of a legal claim could arise.

The International Securities Regulatory Organization (ISRO) is concerned to keep London in the forefront of world financial markets and to regulate international dealing in stocks, shares, bonds, futures, other financial instruments and currencies.

The Institutional Shareholders Committee (ISC) watches the interests of institutional investors. It published a code of practice for directors of public limited companies in April 1991, urging the appointment of more non-executive directors to protect shareholders' interests. Sometimes the formula works and sometimes it doesn't. In the case of ACC during 1982, the non-executive directors proved virtually useless; one former top civil servant resigned just when his analytical mind might have been useful to shareholders.

Enforcement of all the latest legislation obviously necessitates a large central office organization in addition to teams of compliance officers. The

---

[5] By March 1991 it became clear that all was not well with FIMBRA. The basic qualifications for membership (payment of an annual fee, Scotland Yard clearance and no previous bankruptcy) seem hardly adequate to handle people's life savings.

annual cost has been estimated at £100m. It is to be hoped that the growing number of private investors will eventually gain some definite advantage from this expensive and ambitious framework of legal protection.

The London Stock Exchange in its pre-Big Bang form dates from 18 May 1801, when the foundation stone was laid in Capel Court, London EC. The trading floor closed with the Big Bang of 27 October 1986. Now, 1 April 1991 represents yet another significant landmark in the history of London's financial markets.

During 1991 the ISE became the International Stock Exchange PLC eliminating its rule book, substituting the usual memorandum and articles of a PLC, and replacing its council of thirty-two members with a board of twenty-five directors.

The change is not merely technical, it is profound. The ISE moves from being a regulated company to joint stock with limited liability. The history of such regulated companies as the East India and Hudson's Bay Company dates from around 1600.

Clearly, no standard European system of dealing in stocks and bonds will work in the foreseeable future, largely owing to differences in national character. London is gearing up to consolidate its position as Europe's number one financial centre. With a powerful balance of advantage over all continental exchanges in history, tradition, skill, knowledge – and not least in volume of business – London's position as a world financial centre looks set for another big stride forward.

London's financial markets

The framework of financial markets following Big Bang is summarized below: Figure 4 illustrates the relationship between markets and their respective regulatory organizations.

The International Stock Exchange (ISE) – with branches in London, Glasgow, Edinburgh, Belfast and other main towns: the ISE's main market consists of approximately 2700 leading equities which have satisfied the requirement for listing, one of which is that a minimum of 25 per cent of the ordinary share capital is offered for sale through the market. The cost of a full listing is about £600,000. As we have already seen, this market is an electronic market. No trading floor has existed since October 1986.

London International Financial Futures Exchange (LIFFE) is where financial futures are traded (see key to Figure 4). These range from short and long gilts, US Treasury bonds, currency futures such as three-months forward sterling, Euro dollars, dollars, D-marks and the FT-SE 100 Index. Here the minimum contract is much higher – £100,000 for short gilts, for

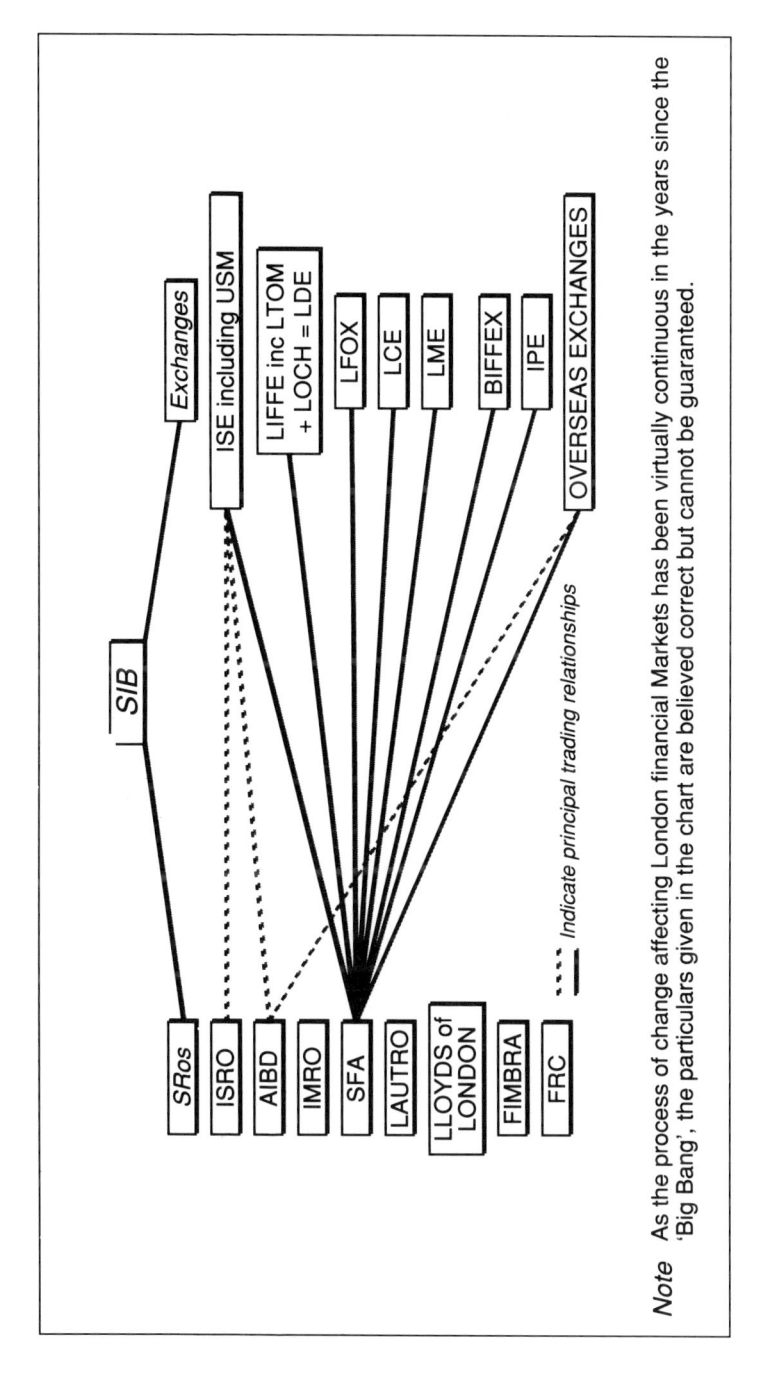

Note As the process of change affecting London financial Markets has been virtually continuous in the years since the 'Big Bang', the particulars given in the chart are believed correct but cannot be guaranteed.

Figure 4, Chart showing the relationship between the Securities and Investment Board, SROs, Exchanges and other related financial bodies as constituted on 1 April 1991

Key to Figure 4

AFBD	Formerly Association of Futures Brokers and Dealers (see SFA).
AIBD	Association of International Bond Dealers.
BIFFEX	Baltic International Freight Futures Exchange.
FIMBRA	Financial Intermediaries and Brokers Regulatory Association. Mainly composed of small firms of investment advisers and insurance brokers.
FRC	Established in 1990 as a new financial reporting council, including an accounting standards board and a review panel to supervise company accounting standards. Financed by government, the accountancy profession, the ISE, via a levy on annual company listing fees, banks, and a further levy on all registered companies. Created to ensure fair presentation of accounts. A company ignoring an ASB ruling can be taken to court by the panel. Directors who have signed accounts ruled unfair by the panel are personally liable for the costs of rectification.
IMRO	Investment Management Regulatory Organization. Mainly large City firms and commercial banks.
IPE	International Petroleum Exchange.
ISE	International Stock Exchange. LTOM now occupies former London Stock Exchange trading floor.
ISRO	International Securities Regulatory Organization. Mainly foreign banks and the International Stock Exchange. It is concerned to keep London in the forefront of world financial markets and to regulate international dealing in stocks, shares, bonds, futures, other financial instruments and currencies.
LAUTRO	Life Assurance and Unit Trust Regulatory Organization.
LCE	London Commodity Exchange.
LFOX	London Futures and Options Exchange.
LIFFE[6]	London International Financial Futures Exchange.
LOCH	London Options Clearing House.
LTOM[6]	London Traded Options Market.
LLOYDS OF LONDON	Fire, Marine, Life and General Insurance.
LME	London Metal Exchange.
SFA	Securities and Futures Authority, incorporating TSA and AFBD from 1 April 1991.
SIB	Securities and Investment Board responsible for co-ordination of SROs and implementation of the Financial Services Act 1986; regulation of Exchanges in UK and certain overseas exchanges.
SROs	Self-regulatory Organizations.
TSA	Formerly The Securities Association regulating the Stock Exchange and certain overseas exchanges. AFBD and TSA merged on 1 April 1991 to become SFA, emphasizing the increasingly close relationship between the cash and futures markets and the financial significance of the fast-expanding futures and options trading. Approximately 700 SFA members out of a total of 1000 are authorized to deal in futures. AFBD is to be wound up by April 1992.
USM	Unlisted Securities Market, incorporating the third market.

---

[6] LIFFE and LTOM merged with effect from 1 April 1991, becoming London Derivatives Exchange – LDE, subsequently amended to LIFFE/LTOM.

example, and £25 per index point for forward contracts on the FT-SE 100 Index, with the LIFFE quotation one-tenth actual. All trades are for cash settlement.

There are important differences both in convention and in trading practice in all financial markets, in addition to variations in contract specifications in the options and futures markets. Investors should familiarize themselves at the outset with trading regulations in the International Stock Exchange rule book and clearly understand the nature and extent of any obligation before it is entered into. While no amount of legislation can prevent investors choosing bad shares or speculating in potentially dangerous futures, it is hoped that closer control and the recent electronic developments will accelerate the general availability of key financial information. Whatever will be, it is reasonably certain that investors in the options and futures markets will require a considerable element of reserved optimism.

Options and futures in rubber, white sugar, cocoa, coffee, are already available on the London Futures and Options Exchange (LFOX). Deliverable contracts for tea and index-based property contracts on commercial property, rents, house prices and mortgage rates started in 1991. The automated trading system, ATS, is being extended to a wide range of futures and options contracts. The US Commodity Futures Trading commission has recently cleared LFOX options to allow trading by US clients.

London Traded Options Market (LTOM) (see key to Figure 4) deals in a relatively new financial instrument, traded options which started in America in 1978 and in Britain in the early 1980s. The market has become established on the former London Stock Exchange trading floor. There are over seventy stocks with a high volume of transactions and volatile price profile making up a single class of traded option. It is also possible to buy traded options in gold, sugar, cocoa, coffee and gas oil and stock index options in the FT-SE 100 Index. The London options clearing house (LOCH) is the mechanism by which settlement is effected. The volume of traded option and traditional option business has shown a marked increase in all classifications since Big Bang.

Economic characteristics of stock markets

Stock markets are often believed to be perfect markets in the model of most commodity exchanges, but this assumption is wildly inaccurate. It is doubtful if any stock market could ever satisfy completely the requirements of a perfect market as defined in economic theory. Those requirements and the extent to which they are met by most organized stock markets are outlined below.

One of the primary requirements of perfect competition is *many buyers, many sellers*. The London market meets this condition for widely traded stocks (alpha and beta categories), but not normally for gamma and never for delta or USM stocks, which are infrequently traded. It is important to note that the larger the market for any share, the closer the price and hence the lower the dealing costs. Widely traded shares should show a more moderate day-to-day fluctuation, in relative terms at any rate, than less frequently traded shares, in accordance with the economic law of markets.

The second fundamental requirement is *one price ruling for the same stock at any one time*. This condition is not met on the London market in respect of any security dealt in. A stockbroker calling up a widely traded – alpha or beta – stock will see displayed on his VDU the three highest bid prices, the middle price and the three lowest asking prices. Each market maker will have set his own dealing prices according to his position in the stock. Market makers learn of all trades via the tape. It is also an exchange requirement that all transactions are reported by brokers within ninety seconds, with detailed notification on the next trading day. These exchange requirements are subject to frequent review and different rules apply for very large transactions.

The third condition is *free exchange of information*. This requirement can never be satisfied on any stock market. Clearly, brokers close to the company and market makers in the share will have the most comprehensive and up-to-date information, which will not be universally available, though the 'bush telegraph' may sometimes extend the range of restricted information. This is particularly true when the shares are said to be 'at an interesting stage'.

A fourth requirement is that *the product shall be homogeneous*, that is, every unit comparable to every other unit of the same class: that every voting share in registered form is equivalent in terms of shareholders' rights to every other share in the same category. Exactly the same situation obtains in the case of bearer stock (extremely rare in Britain), defined as share warrants by section 188 of the Companies Act 1985, where each share warrant is equivalent to every other share warrant. However, registered and bearer forms of shares in the same class are not comparable and there are circumstances in which either one may be preferred. This condition of homogeneity is met on modern stock markets, electronic markets via screen trading and also on so-called telephone markets.

The final condition is that *there should be free entry into the market*. This condition is never met on any exchange, as entry is normally restricted to people of good character and some means, who are introduced by existing members in a similar way to club membership.

It follows that stock markets, operating via floor trading or screen trading, fall well short of the requirements of a perfect market in the pure economic sense. Most exchanges would, however, satisfy the first and fourth conditions in the case of widely traded shares, but the fourth only for all other shares.

3. For Amusement Only

Personalities of the past

There is a speculative element in all business transactions, because profit is the product of risk and uncertainty. It is the high-risk transactions which may be classed as speculative, though, as we have seen, the definition is a difficult one.

Let us now look at the essential characteristics of speculators. The United States is, of course, the land of the speculator; there often seems to be an aggressive, winner-takes-all streak in the American character, a desire to gamble and live dangerously. It is probably true that as many vast fortunes were built on speculation as were ever created by constructive work, and a number of large corporations were put together by entrepreneurs who took enormous risks. Alternatively, like John D. Rockefeller (Standard Oil), 'Commodore' Cornelius Vanderbilt (Harlem, Hudson and New York Central Railroad), or Andrew Carnegie and J. P. Morgan (United States Steel, which controlled 60 per cent of US crude steel production in 1901), they crushed competition to the extent that the government of the day was forced to introduce the Sherman Anti-Trust Law of 1890, intended to block the notorious abuse of power by the great corporations.

Apart from gold, early US stock market speculation had been concentrated in rails and mining stocks. Rail transportation was the key to the development of California and the Middle West, and mining had always possessed its own unique attractions.

The speculator, much more than the investor, needs to stay close to the market, to be able to shift his position quickly in the light of the changing scene. The investor needs to stand back, to be systematic and numerate, a good reader of documents. Both investor and speculator must have that little bit of steel which accepts that all investors lose sometimes. It is interesting to note that failures have more often been the result of a huge speculation having gone seriously wrong than of an investment in the wrong stock. A recent example of this was the attempt to corner the silver market by Texas billionaire Bunker Hunt, resulting in financial ruin.

The demon of stock speculation has been the delight and sometimes the downfall of monarchs, princes and many lesser men. It was said of Lord Clive of India that he never missed an opportunity to take advantage. A reference no doubt to his brilliant military tactics, which greatly advanced British interests in India, but also to his financial strategy which enhanced his personal fortune and those of the directors and shareholders of the East India Company. On his return in the early summer of 1760, he was by common consent reckoned the richest man in England at the age of just thirty-four. Clive had the respect and admiration of both George II and the young George III, though his immense wealth and lavish generosity soon aroused the envy of the East India directors and others in high places.[1]

Prime Minister Sir Robert Walpole's Norfolk home, Houghton Hall near King's Lynn, was said to have been furnished by profits from the South Sea Bubble, and those of Benjamin Disraeli are touched on later. Another Prime Minister, Sir Robert Peel II, sponsor of the 1844 Bank Charter Act, was not, so far as is known, a stock market speculator, though he was a very high stake card player. His father, Sir Robert Peel I, the honourable member for Tamworth and a wealthy Lancashire cotton manufacturer, had answered Pitt's call for financial assistance to continue the war with France. He sent his draft for £10,000 (£300,000 today, prices in 1797 being about one-thirtieth of current levels and 50 per cent above those for 1900). On the death of Sir Robert Peel I in 1830, his estate of £1.4m (£70m at today's values) incurred the highest death duties ever paid in England up to that time.[2] Yet another Prime Minister, A. J. Balfour, and his brother Gerald were substantial stock market investors in high-risk stocks and were said to have jointly lost about £300,000 in a single share speculation.

The Marconi scandal of 1912 implicated both the Prime Minister of the day, David Lloyd George, and the Attorney-General, Sir Rufus Isaacs (later Lord Chancellor as Lord Reading). The managing director of the Marconi Telegraph Company was Godfrey Isaacs, brother of Sir Rufus, and he drew the forthcoming share issue to the attention of the two statesmen. Sir Rufus accepted an allotment of 10,000 shares and Mr Lloyd George 2000 shares, out of Godfrey Isaacs' own allotment of 56,000 $5 shares.[3] Public attention had been alerted to the importance of wireless telegraphy by the Crippen murder case of 1910, which can probably still claim to be *the* case of the twentieth century. In the event, Marconi shares opened at a substantial

---

[1] R. J. Minney, *Clive*, 1935; Sir John Malcolm, *Life of Lord Clive*, 1836.
[2] *The Industrial Revolution in the Eighteenth Century*, Paul Mantoux, 1927.
[3] *FE – A life of F. E. Smith*. Second Earl of Birkenhead, 1965.

premium and this resulted in an indignant press outcry about the financial morality of public men, followed by the inevitable House of Commons enquiry.

Maynard Keynes (1879–1946), the outstanding economist of the twentieth century, was a dangerously enthusiastic investor on margin.[4] He had speculated heavily in commodities, and was virtually insolvent following the postwar market setback of 1921 but, carried by his brokers, he recovered to leave a net estate of £467,000 on his death (approximately £7.5m at today's values). Keynes acknowledged his debt to Irving Fisher (1867–1947), America's leading economic statistician and econometrician of his day. Among Fisher's major works was *The Theory of Interest*, published in 1930. According to J. K. Galbraith, Fisher, the archetypal academic speculator, lost between $8m and $10m in the crash of 1929. This is barely credible, since even at the lower level of losses it represents an estimated $200m at today's values.

Other interesting stock market operators of the 1920s included the father of President John F. Kennedy. Joe Kennedy had sold out in the summer of 1928 and entered the market before the October 1929 crash only as a deadly short sale operator driving the market lower. He was said to have made $100m in property deals in the 1920s and was as ruthless an operator as any latter-day greenmailer.

Of much greater interest to students of investment is Barney Baruch (Union Sulphur), an astute investor in resource companies such as oil, mining, bricks, cement – extremely relevant for today's investors, where a good mining stock is usually a core holding in the portfolio of substantial investors. Two examples of present-day companies following a basic resource philosophy are Lonrho and Hanson. Baruch attached little value to inside information as he believed it tended to block the intellectual process and distort investment decisions which should have been validly made on either fundamental or technical grounds.

Many Hollywood stars were heavy losers in the Wall Street crash of October 1929, none more than Eddie Cantor, a margin speculator who lost the full value of his stock market investments. Cantor's book *Caught Short!*, included the story of the 99-year-old million-dollar investor, impoverished by the crash, who decided to postpone dying until the market improved. Gary Cooper, Lon Chaney, Loretta Young and Adolphe Menjou all suffered large losses.

John Gilbert, who had become Hollywood's premier star of the silent screen after the early death of Valentino in August 1926, found his share

---

[4] See Chapter Seven.

portfolio largely wiped out on his return to the US from a European honeymoon. To make matters worse, another problem was becoming apparent for Gilbert, whose contract with MGM at $250,000 a picture had been last renewed early in 1928. The transition from silent films to talking pictures was proving difficult. Gilbert's gestures and acting style, so well suited to the pantomime of the silent screen, were not right for sound, and there were technical problems associated with his voice. In the event, the introduction of sound on film closed his career in starring roles, together with such famous names as Mary Pickford, John Barrymore, Pola Negri and Ramon Novarro. For John Gilbert this spelt financial ruin.

Winston Churchill, on a visit to America during the late summer of 1929, found his Wall Street investments rather costly. Churchill had returned Britain to the gold standard in 1925 with unfortunate economic consequences, because of the exchange rate which over-valued sterling (paralleled in 1990 by the UK's entry to the exchange rate mechanism [ERM] at £1 = DM2.95).

Hollywood also had its share of successful investors, and while Douglas Fairbanks Snr was managing director, United Artists was always profitable. Bob Hope was named as one of the USA's top fifty richest men by *Fortune* magazine in 1959 with a net worth of around $200m. His main investments were in land and real estate, though he had a shareholding in RCA Records. Mae West was a big Californian land investor during the 1930s. Another astute operator was Western star Randolph Scott, whose eyes never left the stock prices in the *Wall Street Journal* as his stand-in flashed by on the burning coach. William Holden ('Golden Holden') was another wealthy investor.

Actor Edward G. Robinson was a fanatical buyer of paintings, leaving his wife so short of money she could hardly pay the grocery bills – let alone go away on holiday. Robinson left an estate of $3m. Chicago gangster Al Capone, a heavy gambler on the race track, and known to enjoy a high-stake golf game at Lake Shore Drive Chicago, never, so far as is known, bought a share. With an estimated gross annual income of $105m in 1927 one can perhaps see why. Capone, as one of the world's first 'racket executives', was quick to map out an area zoning framework for the city of Chicago, giving himself the larger share of the market. Bootlegging potential should have been based on the location of clubs and bars; the protection racket largely on the location of shops, particularly dry cleaners. Capone used a sales index, probably based on residential population, which was weighted in his favour.[5]

---

[5] *Al Capone*. F. D. Pasley, 1966.

Omar Sharif, actor, ace bridge player and casino owner, reviewing recently a special tabulation of regular patrons' accounts at his casino in France over a twelve-month period, found they were all losers to a man. Amazing, when you consider that roulette odds are only 1.35 per cent in favour of the house on the colours and 2.7 per cent on the numbers.

Distinguished barrister and defence counsel, Sir Edward Marshall Hall, and crime writer Edgar Wallace both enjoyed an investment in an 'interesting situation'. Whittaker Wright, the Victorian financier, whose Globe companies crashed in 1899, was also a promoter of some notorious mining schemes. While working an unsuccessful claim in which he had invested $250,000 at Leadville, Colorado during the great mining boom of 1879, Wright was offered the adjoining claim at a nominal sum, but declined. A few weeks later that claim yielded $600,000. Wright always said he lost two fortunes at Leadville, the one he didn't make on his own claim and the one he would have made on the other.

Ivar Kreuger, the match manufacturer and merger specialist born in Sweden in 1880, became a world financial figure negotiating national loans to post-World War I European nations, including France and Germany, in return for monopoly rights in the production and sale of matches. His financial operations were conducted at the highest level through banking houses such as First National Bank of New York, Deutsche Bank, Crédit Lyonnais and Rothschilds. Apart from his business activities, he was a successful investor on a personal level in stocks and bonds. The famous SELL telegram to associates date-stamped Paris just before his suicide in March 1932, caused heavy falls in the prices of Kreuger and Toll and Swedish Match. K and T, which had touched £56 during 1928 stood at 10p in May 1932. Swedish Match over a similar period had fallen from £26 to 35p.[6]

H. Gordon Selfridge, born in 1858, a partner when he was only thirty in Marshall Field, Chicago, the world's premier retail business of the time, came to London to open his Oxford Street store in March 1909. He bought out a number of other well-known retailers. Closely associated with financier James White (Beecham Trust), Selfridges went public in the late 1920s and subsequently bought Whiteley's of Bayswater, which quickly proved a bad proposition. Gordon Selfridge's personal extravagance and gambling were legendary. He is believed to have squandered £2m between 1929 and 1937 (over £50m at today's values), and by the end of the thirties was in debt to the company. In the early 1940s he resigned the chairmanship in exchange for cancellation of a £118,000 company loan and the nominal title of president, carrying a salary of only £2000 a year.[7]

---

[6] *Ivar Kreuger.* Trevor Allen, 1934.
[7] *No Name on the Door.* A. H. Williams, 1956.

In the summer of 1895, with the boom in South African mining shares at its peak on the London market, Sir Joseph Robinson, an immensely wealthy investor in South African land, diamonds and gold, occupied Dudley House in London's Park Lane. As Mrs Elizabeth Hudson had done at Albert Gate some fifty years earlier, he used society hostesses to entertain his guests. To say that Sir Joseph was not well liked, does not convey an adequate impression of his reputation: it appears that no single act of generosity in word or deed was ever recorded to his credit. On his death in 1929 the *Cape Times* published one of the most virulent obituaries ever compiled.

However, in 1921 Robinson, then an elderly man, had been in contact with Lloyd George regarding the availability of a peerage, presumably offering the list price of £100,000 or maybe negotiating a discount with the Prime Minister, who had been assisted in his own finances by $50,000 from Mr Guggenheim.

Sir Joseph's proposed elevation had been opposed most vigorously and ultimately successfully by Lord Harris, MCC president, a former captain of the England test team and a dominant figure in English cricket for half a century. In any event, the storm broke with the publication of the 1921 Honours List and the South African newspapers were also loud in their condemnation of Robinson, who was already a baronet. He was forced to decline the peerage, afterwards realistically remarking that the honour was not worth the price.

Sir Joseph had long been a supporter of Kruger and in opposition to Rhodes, now dead some twenty years, in everything he had done, facts not calculated to win him popularity in London. Not that Rhodes, a great man by any standards, was a stranger to the intriguing complexities of Victorian finance and the possibilities of considerable financial advantage for the successful company promoter. Robinson was not only every bit as wealthy as Rhodes, but was insatiably greedy and mean spirited. He had been fined a record £500,000 by the South African courts for a sale and repurchase manipulation of Randfontein stock. One point perhaps in Sir Joseph's favour was that his character never changed; he made no attempt at public generosity late in life to square his account with destiny.[8]

John D. Rockefeller, on the other hand, that notorious abuser of corporate power in the form of his Standard Oil Trust, and the world's richest man in his day, founded Chicago University in 1889. What a pity he did not also contribute a short monograph for the university library on

---

[8] *Statesmen, Financiers & Felons.* The Marquess of Winchester, 1936; *Rhodes.* Lockhart and Woodhouse, 1963.

price discrimination as a legitimate competitive device, to stand alongside other works in that sector of managerial economics. Al Capone also clearly understood the pricing mechanism, but thought the odds against stock market investment far too high. Nevertheless, for all Capone's unpleasant characteristics (he was never charged with murder, only tax evasion), he extended many a financial helping hand to those who fell on hard times and contributed to the soup kitchens set up in Chicago during the hard winters of the 1920s.[9]

Perhaps the final word on financial personalities should go to one of the most exciting adventurers of modern times, who combined entrepreneurial skill with vision and political ambition. Cecil Rhodes was the founder of two great mining corporations, De Beers and Consolidated Goldfields, as well as the British South Africa Company, which shaped the commercial destiny of Rhodesia (now Zimbabwe) after its charter was granted on 29 October 1889. He masterminded the abortive Jameson Raid of 1895 from the Johannesburg offices of Consolidated Goldfields in a desperate attempt to extend British influence in southern Africa. He was Prime Minister of Cape Colony while pursuing his normal commercial interests, had a country named after him, envisaged the Cape to Cairo Railway (which never came about), and died at the early age of forty-nine in 1902, leaving an estate of just over £4m (£180m at today's values).

In 1874, South African laws restricting the transfer and ownership of all types of mining claim were repealed, which cleared the way for speculators and particularly for Rhodes whose financial success derived from astutely buying out competitors including the flamboyant diamond speculator Barney Barnato. Rhodes realized that capital-intensive deep mining of diamonds and gold was the key to success. He increased the size of his operations by consolidating a series of claims so that he was soon able to raise capital on the London market. He was said to despise his investors, who had a long wait for dividends, and he never attended company meetings.[10]

Finally, it is perhaps interesting to observe that South Africans in general seem to have a more cautious commercial approach than that found in other mining countries such as the United States, Canada, Mexico and Australia. South Africa is the home of the mining finance house, whereby risks are spread through cross-holdings of shares and joint ventures in individual projects. This co-operative risk-sharing in mining is virtually non-existent outside South Africa.

---

[9] Pasley, *op. cit.*
[10] Lockhart and Woodhouse, *op. cit.; Consolidated Goldfields*. Paul Johnson, 1987. Rhodes' grave is at World's View, Zimbabwe, thirty miles south-west of Bulawayo.

Investor profiles of today

The object of these snapshot pictures of a variety of stock market investor classifications is to give new investors an insight into the character and personalities of some of the more experienced players. Many of the composites are based on individuals within the writer's personal knowledge, but they have been disguised to avoid embarrassment.

It is obviously possible to classify investors in a number of ways. We may separate them by age and experience or according to their knowledge of the subject, by the size of their average transaction or their net worth. Again, we could identify the type of shares held, reflecting attitude to risk, or whether their approach is analytical, instinctive, systematic or random. In the event, I have used a mixed form of classification to highlight the extreme variety of the investor population.

The new investor
- Age range: 25–45
- Occupation: Any
- Information sources: Television; *Daily Mail*; *Daily Telegraph*
- Agent: Bank
- Typical shares: British Telecom, Anglian Water, Shell Transport and Trading
- Intention: To extend his or her knowledge, to widen information sources and build up a portfolio

The punter (amateur)[11]
- Age range: 25–60
- Typical occupations: Sales rep; pro-golfer; footballer, snooker or darts player; airline pilot; taxi driver; leisure facility operator; motor trader; business consultant; showbiz or TV personality; market trader; publican, etc.
- Agent: Bank; stockbroker
- Information sources: Market tips; television; newsletters; newspapers (basically a non-reader)
- Intention: To make a killing and retire to Spain
- Note: Seems to do everything wrong, but occasionally comes up with a winner, against the odds

The punter or speculator (professional), incorporating the account trader

Professional investors in this category include the bull who buys shares hoping for an immediate price rise to be able to resell at a profit. It also

---

[11] See definition in glossary.

includes the bear, or short sale specialist, who, detecting a market weakness, sells shares he doesn't own hoping to cover his sale at a lower price before settlement. The bull and the bear are usually account traders, thus halving commissions on sale and purchase. Their operations will be much more difficult when the four-day account replaces the existing ten working days plus ten-day settlement system.

The stag is another stock market 'creature' frequently encountered. He applies for a large allocation of a new issue hoping it will open at a premium and thus yield a quick profit.

Then there is the swing trader, a speculator who makes a detailed study of market trends. He or she buys a share when it is seen to be below trend, having fallen to the support level which brings in buyers. The swing trader sells when it rises above trend to its resistance level, causing short-term holders to sell.

Finally, there is the situations investor or arbitrageur, who takes large lines of stock in recovery situations or shares with early takeover possibilities (deal stocks). As he is buying in hundreds of thousands or even millions, his information will be the best. While the amateur hopes to make a profit, the professional systematically cleans up substantial profits, and the arbitrageur aims to win it all.

Information sources:	Newspapers including the *Financial Times*; brokers' circulars; stock market letters; exchange of information with other operators; Extel cards; ShareWatch, stockbroking connections on international markets

The small investor; the middle investor

Age range:	25+
Occupation:	Any
Agent:	Bank (small investor); broker (middle investor)
Information sources:	Television; newspapers; stock market newsletters (small investor company accounts); middle investor will take *Financial Times* and use Extel Card Service and also receive stockbrokers' circulars in addition to company accounts
Range of transaction size:	£500–£7500 (small investor) £10,000–£50,000 (middle investor)
Typical shares:	British Gas, Southern Water, TSB, ICI (small investor); RTZ, Lonrho, Hanson, Lasmo, Storehouse, Polly Peck, Next, Bridon, Readicut (middle investor)

The executive investor
Age range: 35–65
Agent: Broker (senior and middle executives)
Information sources: *Financial Times*; club; stockbroker
Shares: May invest in shares of company he works for, and share option schemes available for senior executives; also in companies or industries in which previously employed or in trade suppliers or customers

Tax-oriented investor

The tax-oriented investor is often a qualified accountant, civil servant, local government officer or schoolmaster. Always looking for low yield, high quality stocks, often reinvesting dividends or taking stock in lieu of dividends. Loves bed-and-breakfast deals, capital gains calculations involving loss indexation and part disposals combining a mix of equity and convertible loan stock. Often keeps ledgers of his fifty-seven separate holdings. Enjoys all the tedious detail of PEP with its minimal investment advantage. Is now into BES, expounding the taxation advantages and good capital gains potential. Frankly, he or she has the full sympathy of the writer for all the hard work and effort, usually for mediocre results, whether measured short, medium or long term. May not make a million, but will hardly ever suffer a serious loss.

The intellectual investor, including computer buffs

Often university professors, lecturers or computer fanatics. Academics are often over-analytical, love market gossip, and sometimes plunge heavily into unbelievably risky mining ventures or commodity futures. May have a substantial portfolio; normally shrewder and often much wealthier than they may wish to appear.

The computer buff thinks his latest machine has all the answers and that prices, resistance and support levels are statistically predictable within exceedingly fine limits. On a rising market these people can do very well. In difficult and volatile conditions you never hear of them.

The ethical investor

Invests according to personal beliefs and principles. This could certainly apply to a very large number of investors, who do not wish to profit from areas of commerce they see as undesirable. The ultimate ethical investors would not invest in South African shares, or in tea or rubber plantation shares or mining stocks involving worker exploitation. If they were against abortion they would avoid London International; against tobacco, BAT; against pollution, ICI; against defence spending, Vickers or VSEL.

Obviously, there will still be many good investment opportunities available to the ethical investor, but this additional constraint increases the difficulty of share selection and of maximizing return on capital.

Some women investors

(i) *Widows and divorcees*: the widow or divorcee with money to invest must look for solid, long-term value: good income stocks with no problems. The divorcee with a sum available for investment following the divorce needs good, genuine advice from bank or broker. They should avoid speculative stocks, start-up propositions and taking a financial interest in the business of a friend, unless well established and then only after having a verification of the investment by a completely independent adviser. They should not shrink from paying for unbiassed financial advice; doing without it can be far more dangerous.

A widow's investments may be those of her late husband and, if they are sound, there may be a good case for retaining the portfolio largely unchanged. Again, professional advice is needed. A case recently judged in the US courts shows how deadly 'churning' a portfolio can be where a broker has been given discretion. A widow had been left a $500,000 share portfolio as part of her husband's estate, which was then placed in the hands of a leading firm of stockbrokers to manage with full discretion. At the end of four years the value of the portfolio had halved to $250,000 and the broker's commission had amounted to the same figure. The judge reached the conclusion that the widow's portfolio had been churned and awarded her the total broker's earnings from her account as damages, thus reinstating her capital at its original level of $500,000. Regretting he could not award her a higher figure, the judge noted that if the portfolio had been left unchanged its value at the time of the court action would have exceeded $700,000.

(ii) *The executive woman*

Age range:	25–45
Occupation:	Accountant; solicitor; business economist; market researcher; any professional, managerial or executive occupation
Information sources:	*Telegraph; Times; Independent*; television; published accounts of employing company
Agent:	Bank
Investments:	Building society; high interest bank account; company share scheme; privatization stocks; PEP,[12] ICI, Glaxo

[12] The 1990 Budget increased the limit to £6000, with a maximum of £3000 in unit or investment trusts. The 1991 Budget permitted an investment of £3000 in a single share and allowed employee shares to be transferred into a personal equity plan (PEP) at no expense to the holder, increasing the limit to £9000.

Intention:	Wants to move her investment knowledge up a notch. Would like to buy more exciting shares like, Lasmo Ops, Barratt, Lonrho, Rustenberg, Impala, etc.
Note:	Needs to research more widely than her present texts, to examine *Financial Times* and Extel cards, and to exchange views with fellow executive investors.

The wealthy investor; the entrepreneurial investor

Age:	30+
Occupations:	Builders; farmers/landowners; large hoteliers and proprietors of large rest and nursing homes; property owners/developers; film or TV stars; best-selling authors; barristers; film producers; surgeons
Information sources:	*Financial Times;* company accounts; stockbrokers
Agent:	Stockbroker
Shares/Investments:	Mining stocks; oils; speculative stocks; Eurotunnel; Eurodisney; traded options; commodity futures; stock index options; privatizations; US/Japanese stocks
Net worth:	£3m+
Note:	Some of these investors will have a large part of their fortune in the market and will be active players. Others, often entrepreneurs, simply have a marginal interest in the odd speculative stock such as Eurotunnel.

Serious investors, fundamental and technical; the hyperactive investor; the investor (retired)

Age range:	35+
Occupation:	Any
Information sources:	Newspapers including the *Financial Times;* newsletters; stockbrokers' circulars; company accounts.

The serious investor selecting shares on fundamentals – that is to say on the basic factors such as earnings per share (EPS), PE ratio, dividend growth, cover, debt/equity ratio, etc. – is looking for value in the shape of good growth yield of income plus capital appreciation in the medium (eighteen months – three years) and long term (three years and more). Also interested in takeover and recovery situations, government privatizations. Not interested in traded options, futures or stock index options. The serious technical investor has the same ends in view, but accepts the proposition that a graphical representation of recent share price movements forms a sound basis for predicting further movements. While the statistical validity of this assumption is problematic, the pattern of share price movements and numbers of trades (sales or purchases) undoubtedly discloses vital information about the existing technical position of a stock. Technical analysis is in effect the study of short-term share price movements, fundamental analysis the study of medium and longer term expectations (see Chapter Seven). The investor who feels attracted to the technical approach should realize at the outset that it involves much more work than studying fundamentals.

A word about the hyperactive investor: this is someone who buys and sells on impulse and rumour, is unsystematic and cannot be bothered to analyse a situation. Believes their guess is as good as the next person's. Unfortunately, that is unlikely to be the case. A friend of their stockbroker, he or she is frequently in the stockbroker's office; in essence a punter.

The investor (retired) is usually a person of considerable investment experience, often with a substantial portfolio, whose transactions have been at a standstill for some years. He will join in investment discussions, but is no longer active, buying nothing and selling nothing. By implication, he has come to terms with the fact that if he dies at the top of the cycle he will leave his widow a substantial fortune, but if at the bottom of the cycle her future will be much less secure.[13] Clearly, a standstill policy avoids the damaging consequences of churning, but is not to be recommended. Rights and new issue opportunities will be missed, also, for example, major developments in Eastern European and South African markets following the present political reforms – not to mention the valuable annual capital gains exemptions.

A financial discussion

Few conversational openings can match the dramatic impact of the stock market tip. Yet stock market conversations, until recently, have often been confined to a knowledgeable inner circle. Indeed, one more classification of individuals in general might be the distinction between those who have shares and know about them and those who do not. Whatever people may say, there are not many subjects of greater interest than money. And as Sir J. G. McDonald explains in his sympathetic *Rhodes – A Life*, it is not so much a vast amount of money that fascinates, it is more the use that is made

---

[13] The assumption that a man will predecease his wife is statistical, based on the fact that there are in Great Britain approximately twice as many women over eighty alive as there are men.

of it that grips us, as well as providing vital clues to the inner personality of its possessor.

The following conversation among a group of club golfers, who are also active investors, is fictional and offered with the disclaimer that any similarity or apparent reference to persons living or dead is purely coincidental.

'I must call my broker on Monday,' said the major. 'I want to take a profit on Lasmo.'

'I see spot crude prices are moving up smartly after the severe winter,' said Vic. 'Still you can't go wrong taking a profit, I suppose.'

'I took a bath on Dixons,' grunted John. 'In at 173p, now a lousy bid of 120p from Kingfisher – bid referred to the MMC[14] fortunately. I don't like the stock either,' he grumbled, 'but they must be worth more than 120p.'

'Why buy them if you didn't like them?' asked the judge rhetorically. 'I'm enjoying Anglian and Welsh Water; the most refreshing drinks I've had for years!'

'I got a good allocation of Mickey Mouse shares[15] and I've piled into Eurotunnel at 375p and the warrants at 34p,' said George, whose steel-grey Bentley stood elegantly in the car park.

'All right for you,' moaned Freddie. 'You've got it made, chum. Seriously, though, both those shares are real punters' stocks, with no payout for years and maybe never.' Not for widows and orphans.

'I agree,' smiled George, 'but as you know, Freddie, I do have a strong predilection for the speculative share with a little bit of interest. Anyway, I must get some drinks in before I go. What would you like?'

'I like shares that keep on riding, just like Randolph Scott in those old Westerns,' said Mike. 'I nominate Lonrho as a share for all seasons,' he said almost defiantly (nods of approval and some groans from Neville, a former holder of Ashanti Mines). 'Though I would never have bought them if I had just relied on the *Daily Mail*. That paper never has a good word to say for them, no matter how good the results. Anyway they keep on paying good dividends.'

'What do some of these people know about shares?' said Arthur. 'They never have shares. Incidentally, I made a nice little killing on 10,000 Connells[16] in the Christmas Account of 1989 – in at 161p and out at 195p.'

'Must be insider trading,' mused the major reflectively.

---

[14] Monopolies and Mergers Commission.
[15] Eurodisney.
[16] A reference to the Luton estate agents taken over by Scottish Widows in July 1990.

'No, sir,' said Arthur, ruffled, 'I don't listen at keyholes, and I've got no City contacts other than my broker. I'm a transaction-only client so I get no advice from him.'

I did it my way . . . an appalling imitation of the famous Sinatra number is heard from the bar.

'I'm thinking of taking stock in lieu of dividends on my Ocean Transport and Marley,' said Dickie.

'Well, I am surprised,' said Arthur. 'This is just another corner shot by firms trying to avoid paying out cash and often of saving non-recoverable ACT; Lonrho is doing it now. I'll consider taking shares for dividends when the directors pay themselves in the company's paper and not before,' he added cynically.

'I must say I like Powell Duffryn at 275p with a PE of 9.6 against the Transport Sector average of 13,' said Eddie. 'They must be a cheap share now, having been up to 351p earlier in the year.'

'Catch a falling star,' mused the major.

'With a yield of 9.6 they could be a nice share for the ladies,' added Ed.

'What does that ridiculous observation mean?' asked Laurie.

'Well,' said Eddie, the club's unofficial technical expert, 'knowledgeable women investors are much more dividend oriented than men, usually looking for solid value not flash in the pan third market, or should we say USM, hi-tech or Eldorado mining stocks.'

'Okay professor, we get the message,' replied Laurie, wishing he hadn't asked.

Archie the steward was clearing the lunch-time glasses, and the slam of the expanding steel shutters on the bar brought to a close another edition of shareholder's question time.

4. Aspects of Risk

A working definition of risk might be the possibility of incurring financial loss or misfortune. The misfortunes of everyday life need not detain us, as everyone is well aware of, say, travel risks and those of illness or disease. Once we come to the chance of incurring financial loss, there is a watershed separating two distinct classes of risk – insurable risks and those business and other risks which for one reason or another are not insurable.

Insurable risks are all those – fire, accident, marine, life, motor, etc., which insurance companies undertake in return for the payment of premiums. For example, the owner-occupier of a house worth £100,000 wanting to insure against fire, storm and flood damage, will be quoted a premium based on the insurer's assessment of those risks. This would take account of the location of the building; a house located in a high flood risk area would pay a higher premium or have flood risk excluded. It would also consider the construction of the building (thatched roofs carry higher premiums), its age, whether it is detached, semi-detached or terraced. It would also take into account any previous claims experience of the proposer. Insurance companies have access to ordnance survey and other large-scale maps (50 inch=1 mile) in dense urban areas, which show individual buildings and in some cases the purposes for which they may be used. In America, such maps are known as the Sanborn maps, and incorporate much greater detail of interest to insurers than any generally available in Britain.

Finally, the insurer will take account of the area where a house is located. Great Britain has been classified into postcode areas and districts since 1975,[1] and insurers apply a risk factor to postcode districts according to

---

[1] *Postcode Marketing Gazetteer of Britain*, E. B. Groves, 1989.

their claims experience. For example, PE30 (Hunstanton, Norfolk) is classified 1, whereas London SW5 (Earl's Court), SW9 (Brixton/Stockwell) and SE19 (Crystal Palace) are all classified with the highest risk index of 6. Perhaps surprisingly, BN1–BN2 (Brighton) falls in the same classification as Orkney (KW15–KW17) with a classification of only 2.

In the field of motor insurance risks are classified by type of vehicle, where garaged, age, occupation of the owner, and by type of use. Again, as many motorists will know, the term comprehensive is not all it might seem, particularly in connection with a loss arising where a motorist is induced to part with his car by a trick. Larceny by trick, technically theft, usually leaves the motorist, not the insurer, suffering the loss.

All insurance companies maintain extensive statistical records and exchange information with other insurers. Life assurance is a further example of a predictable risk insurance companies accept subject to full disclosure by the insured.

In many aspects the insurance business is not so different from that of a bookie who lays odds of 3 to 1 against the favourite. He says, in effect, you have in my book one chance in four of winning. If you place a £10 bet and your horse wins, I will pay you £30 plus your stake money returned. For the mathematically minded this may be expressed so that the expectation (E) of winning is equal to that of losing, i.e. a fair bet; the expectation of winning plus the expectation of losing = 0. Hence $E(win)(£10) \; 3 \times (1/4) + E(lose)(-£10) \; 3/4 = 0$.

Non-insurable risks extend across the whole spectrum from the possibility of loss arising from house purchase where a location is blighted by subsequent development, to the contingent liability undertaken when putting up bail for someone or signing a bank guarantee.

No purpose would be served here by a more detailed look into such everyday obligations and the risks arising from them, except perhaps where they fall within the scope of trade or business. Here it is clear that a young, inexperienced person starting a small business with limited capital[2] is at

---

[2] Rent review clauses in commercial leases need careful study and often expert advice. The inexperienced buyer of a trading business should also note that accounts will, on average, be six or seven months out of date, so he or she should ask for a certificate of turnover from those same accountants to a date as close as possible to the handover. Turnover can slip away quickly in the face of fierce competition these days. The prospective buyer should always use an *independent stocktaker*, as otherwise he would be placed at a disadvantage when dealing with the experienced vendor of the business. Where a business is sold as a going concern, no VAT is payable on stock transferred. The purchaser should also check carefully any assets on HP or leased, to verify any obligations he may be assuming. This may require specialist help, because once the deal is done, matters have to stand. The business is either value for money or it is not.

much greater risk than someone more experienced in the ways of the world, and with some reserve of capital behind him.

Information from debt agencies regarding business failures tells us that two of the main current causes of financial failure are high interest rates and cash flow problems. Excessive expenditure on advertising and promotion and bad accounting are also often cited as contributory factors. An analysis by type of business failure may often prove of interest: small builders, grocers and wool shops figure prominently. The risk of business failure – apart from bad debts insurance and loss of profits insurance following fire or storm damage – is uninsurable. The variability of business risk, by its nature, does not lend itself to a standard statistical treatment and no meaningful premiums could ever be quoted.

Limited liability, as we have seen in Chapter One, can in certain circumstances give protection to a small operation, though not from reckless trading by the directors. However, as we have also noted, most of the risks of commercial misfortune are never insurable, though stock market investors may receive a measure of assistance from recent legislation, as mentioned earlier.

Investment risks of different corporate securities

It is clear that different shares will have different risks for investors. A small start-up proposition will carry an inherently high risk, whereas shares in a large, well-established company should, if purchased at the right price, constitute a relatively low-risk investment. Few serious investors would claim they always spot the winners, and that is why a spread of investment is so vital. Perhaps five shares out of ten show growth yield – income plus capital growth; two are at a standstill, paying dividends only; and two or three are losers, having gone ex-growth. This might be a typical portfolio of the low handicap investor.

Trendy stocks have a high profile and might sound exciting, but they are often too expensive to meet the experienced investor's basic growth yield requirements.

Here is a summary of the principal types of stock market security with an indication of the risk attached to them:

Security	Risk rating	Return
Debentures	Low. A debenture holder is a secured creditor of the company and receives payment before all other securities. Usually a fixed	Interest

	or floating charge on a company's assets. The debenture holder may be more interested in the security of net asset value than the ordinary shareholder.	
Preference shares	Moderate. Dividends payable before ordinary shareholders. Most preference shares are cumulative – that is any arrears of dividends are payable before ordinary shareholders can receive any dividends.	Dividends
Preferred ordinary shares	Moderate. These shares lie in an intermediate position between preference and ordinary shares, often conferring participation in profits and sometimes residual rights in a winding-up.	Dividends
Ordinary shares	Variable from low to very high risk, depending upon size and nature of company and the amount of loan capital to service (gearing). However, one company's ordinary shares may be a better security than another company's debentures secured by a floating charge. Ordinary shares may be issued in registered or bearer form, the former being the common practice in Britain. Bearer stocks are negotiable securities with title passing by delivery and have a sheet of coupons attached for future dividend payments, known as share warrants.	Dividends
'A' shares	As for ordinary shares, but carry no voting rights which can be a problem for holders in a takeover situation.	Dividends
Deferred shares	Unusual, high-risk security. Receive dividends after all other types of capital have been paid. Of mainly historical interest.	Dividends
Convertible loan stock	Moderate. Gives a fixed interest return and carries a future right to convert to ordinary shares at a predetermined rate.	Interest until conversion, then dividends

Debenture and loan stock holders are creditors. Shareholders are members of the company, whose investment remains in the company for the whole of its existence or until they sell or transfer the shares. Preference shares and preferred ordinary shares normally vote only when dividends are in arrears.

One of the great advantages a well-chosen ordinary share possesses over a fixed interest bond such as British Government gilt edged, is that it offers a shield against the fixed interest investor's nightmare of high inflation.

It is certain that there can be no such thing as an investment without risk, as many gilt-edged investors can testify. For example, during 1948 the average dividend yield on industrial ordinary shares of 5.16 per cent was greater than the average return on 2½ per cent Consols (3.21 per cent),

Table 2 UK ordinary share prices and retail prices with equivalent buying powers of £1 for selected years (1890–1990), with retail prices projected for 2000

Year	Ordinary share price index[1] (annual averages) (1958=100)	Index of Retail prices[1] (1890=100)	Value of £1
1890	21	100	100p[2]
1900	24	102	98p
1914	23	117	85p
1920	39	255	39p
1931	33	170	59p
1938	46	179	56p
1958	100	483	21p
1970	452	714	14p
1980	501	2671	4p
1990	1925	4915	2p
2000 (projected)[3]		8011	1¼p

Notes:

1. London and Cambridge Economic Service and other sources.

2. All values expressed in new pence equivalents: 100p = 240d = £1.

3. Assumes average annual rate of inflation of 5 per cent compound between 1990 and 2000.

leaving a yield gap of +1.95 per cent, because the risks of possessing shares were considered greater than the risk of holding Consols and inflation was not a major factor. The general price level in Britain had fallen in the inter-war years of 1919–1938 by approximately 30 per cent. From 1944 to 1961 prices virtually doubled and this brought about a change in investor attitudes to fixed interest stock and the emergence of the 'reverse yield gap'. This meant that the yield on gilts now stood above that on ordinary shares because of the inflation factor. For example, during 1961 the average yield on industrials was 5.34 per cent and that on 2½ per cent Consols 6.20 per cent – a reverse or negative yield gap of –0.86 per cent.

Investors with an interest in price movements of ordinary shares in the aggregate and of retail prices in Britain over the past 100 years may find the approximations of ordinary share prices and of retail price levels, together with related purchasing powers of a £ for selected years, of some relevance for general reference purposes (Table 2).

The table shows an approximate rise in excess of 4800 per cent over 100 years to 1990. The equivalent internal buying power of £1 has fallen to a close approximation of 2p over the same period.[3] The acceleration of inflationary pressure during the final twenty years (1970–1990) has had a considerable impact on incomes and the net values of estates.

A prewar annual income of £2000 needs about £54,000 in 1990 to maintain equivalent buying power, leaving aside differences in tax rates and house prices. In London and the south east, incomes in excess of this figure are commonplace, but while many will have exceeded the total inflation from 1938 to 1990 of twenty-seven times 1938 price levels, others will not have done so. However, if an accurate index of house prices were available for London and the south east covering that period, average current house prices would surely register well in excess of 100 times their 1938 levels, with typical current mortgage interest rates at four to five times the prewar average of around 3 per cent.

In such high-income residential districts in Greater London as Hampstead, Kensington, Highgate, Richmond, Wimbledon and Enfield, house prices exceeding 300 times prewar values can be readily instanced. Thus the £500,000 London and south east home may become far more commonplace during the 1990s.

---

[3] It may be of interest for some readers to note the course of the international value of the £ sterling over a similar period, since foreign exchange provides us with an index of international currency values. Taking the £1/$ closing sight rate for 7 December 1907 (*Banking and Currency*, Ernest Sykes, 1918) from *The Times* as £1 =$ 4.8615 and the closing rate for 19 March 1991 from the *Financial Times* of 20 March 1991 of £1 = $1.7650, the dollar value of the £ sterling has fallen by approximately 65 per cent over a period close to five-sixths of a century.

Householders paying the current (1991) murderous rates of mortgage interest may sometimes wonder why this purely domestic interest rate must be so inflexibly coupled to international rates and the external value of sterling, when both borrowers and virtually all lenders are UK residents.

South Africa provides us with a current example of a dual exchange rate, of importance to investors in Kaffirs (South African gold shares). Assuming a UK investor had decided on 3 January 1990 to invest in Goldfields of South Africa 10 cents Ordinary, he would have had to purchase South African rands at the commercial rate of exchange ruling on that day, R(cm)4.1450 = £1. His broker should have advised him that the dividend yield shown in the *Financial Times* of 10.4 per cent represents the gross return to a South African *resident investor*. Dividend income remitted to the UK will be converted at the financial rate of exchange, which for 3 January 1990 was R(fn)5.6955 = £1. This reduces a UK investor's return on a South African share to 7.56 per cent, since (4.1450/5.6955 × 10.40 = 7.56 per cent); a reduction of nearly 27 per cent on the FT quoted nominal yield of 10.4 per cent.

What's happened to gilts?

In the last few years the British government has pursued a policy of Public Sector Debt Repayment (PSDR). Trading in gilts has been restricted, and the practical effect is that gilt-edged prices and yields no longer automatically react to changes in prevailing Bank of England base rates. For example, a 15 per cent official base-rate ruling during the first two months of 1990 saw average redemption yields on gilts – shorts(up to 5 years) 11.75 per cent; mediums(5–15 years) 10.75 per cent; and longs(over 15 years) 10 per cent.

It may be noteworthy for the fixed interest investor that when the yields of a selection of gilts are plotted on a chart by reference to their redemption dates, the result is a yield curve. Figure 5 which depicts approximate actual and projected yields over the period 1979–2006, supplies an example of a 'humped yield'. Interest rates rise to a peak in 1981, fall to 1989, with a slight rise in 1990 and a longer-term fall thereafter. As with all forecasts, the projections are best estimates at the date of compilation (January 1990).

As we have seen, the rise in general interest rates did not result in a corresponding adjustment in gilt-edged yields. Thus the possibility (existing until the end of 1982) for a stock market investor to move into gilts on a sharp rise in rates and a corresponding fall in gilt prices, selling when interest rates fell and gilt-edged prices moved up, has been effectively closed by the official PSDR policy. This policy has introduced, in effect, a technical distortion into the now declining gilt-edged market.

The investment time frame

Fun investments

It is sometimes said that no one is in business for his or her health, but this commercial generalization will not stand too much scrutiny. For example, a substantial businessman may well finance his wife or daughter in an enterprise which could in no sense be regarded as economically viable.

Again, investors known as 'angels' put up cash to stage very high-risk theatrical productions.[4] The Blue Arrow £25m investment in Peter de Savory's operation, made without reference to interest, share of profit or repayment terms, surely falls within this category, judging by the fact that Manpower, the US-based employment service company which subsequently bought control of Blue Arrow, has written the £25m down to a nominal $1 in its books.

Film production, publishing and the making of sound recordings are well up in the highest category of business risk and they have given birth to some of the most exciting enterprises. Warner Brothers gave the cinema-going public an absorbing interest and occasionally the thrill of a lifetime plus value for money with so many of their low-budget, high-impact films during the 1930s, 1940s and 1950s.[5] They correctly anticipated the big potential for sound in 1927 with their landmark production of the first talking picture, *The Jazz Singer*, using their Vitaphone system. MGM, Paramount and Universal hesitated, but by the end of 1929 more than 9000 cinemas in the US had installed the new sound system.

Boomtowns

Curiously, the economic characteristics of the boomtown featured in so many Hollywood productions are strikingly similar to those of a wave of stock market speculation which subsides with a crash. In a typical boomtown scenario based on a mining discovery, such as diamonds in Kimberley in 1870, gold in Colorado in 1879 or in California in 1849, only a very few strike it rich. The rest are mostly unlucky losers, excluding those who provide services to the prospectors (speculators), such as banking, clothing and footwear, food and drink, hardware, transport, etc. As more people arrive, local prices move up sharply. Even a small discovery encourages additional fortune hunters from afar, which strains the local

---

[4] Such investments are usually non-transferable and are required to comply with the Financial Services Act 1986.
[5] *The Warner Brothers Story.* Clive Hirschhorn, 1980.

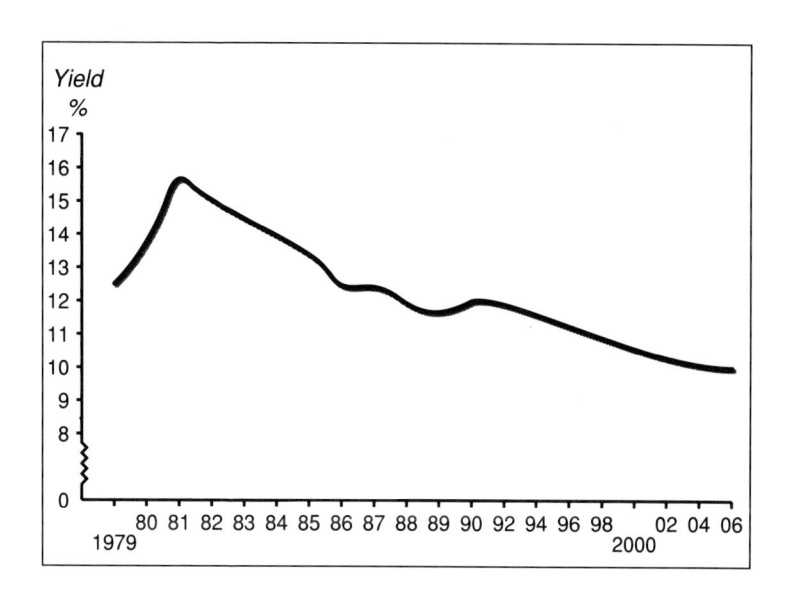

Figure 5, Chart showing a yield curve comprising typical redemption yields on short-term gilts for 1979–89; also yields on short, medium and long gilts to 2006

economy even more, whipping prices up to still higher levels. Eventually there is the general realization that the fortune sought is illusory and that most people won't strike pay dirt, since more money has been sunk in gold mining than ever came out of it. Business activity declines, some investments are totally lost and the caravan moves on.

Very similar conditions obtained in the Florida land boom of the 1920s, where there was excessive subdivision of land to maximize developers' profits. Still, people kept on buying; bricks and mortar are always the best investment, aren't they? So prices kept rising, until by 1926 it dawned on investors that they were not buying value. Confidence was shaken and the boom collapsed, leaving the inevitable trail of puzzled losers.

London and Aberdeen during the 1970s and 1980s may indeed be cited as latter-day examples of boomtowns in the housing sense. The London and south east market received a serious setback in 1988, when the government withdrew multiple mortgage interest relief for people jointly buying a residential property. Just before the withdrawal of this tax break in August 1988, mortgage interest rates had started to move up until they had almost doubled, increasing from 7.9 per cent to 15.4 per cent over the period May 1988 to March 1989.

People late into any speculative situation are always the biggest losers in the subsequent crash. And there nearly always is a crash or some sharp setback when any market overheats.

Short- and medium-term investments

Before looking at short-term investments in general, we may briefly mention traded options, traditional options, index betting and futures, which are dealt with in more detail in Chapter Seven. These are all investments which will show a definite financial result either one way or another within a given time scale or at a prearranged future date.

The stock market investor will select the time frame most suited to his financial aims and his personality: up to six months may be considered short. The situations investor, for example, is essentially a short-term thinker, and his time scale for a particular investment may be as brief as a single stock exchange account, since carrying charges for such investments are so high.

A medium-term investment is expected to show a profit within six to twenty-four months. A long-term investment may be termed one which needs at least two years to generate the anticipated return. The difference between the short- and the longer-term is not only the obvious one of timing but also a difference in the nature of the investment and the outlook of the investor.

Whatever time frame the investor is most happy in (and sometimes it may be a series of distinct types of investment proposition, all with quite different timings) will usually show the best results. Most private investors are neither share traders nor situations investors. They buy shares to hold, and will often put up with a good deal of disappointment before parting with a particular share. Further, some shares can become a friend for life, receiving the private investor's supreme accolade.

Time share

No account of investment opportunities of this era could be considered adequate without some reference to time-share investments. As the description suggests, they are not really an investment in any sense whatever, simply the purchase of a fraction, say one-fiftysecond or two-fiftyseconds of a long leasehold holiday apartment, often with low-grade free golf and other leisure facilities.[6] For the sophisticated individual, time share may be perfectly satisfactory, but not such a good idea for the marginal investor, who has not perhaps fully grasped the concept and for whom subsequent fluctuations in air travel expense, in the case of overseas developments, and service charges in all time-share deals, might be major factors.

Managed investments

The matter of managed investment need not detain us long. For many people the managed approach, via bank or stockbroker or by unit trust investment, is the right one. With effect from 1 January 1991 the Securities and Investment Board (SIB) has authorized unit trust investment in property, options and futures, which considerably increases the risk factor for this type of investment. Again, estates inherited by young people under-age or in some cases held in trust until the beneficiary reaches twenty-five years of age, clearly require experienced, high integrity, long-term management.

Investing for the longer term

The nature of certain long-term investments has already been mentioned, and a case can frequently be made out for investing in a share whose market is in long-term decline. The rate of decline is frequently over-estimated by analysts, and the share's prospects thus downgraded. In many instances, the struggle for market percentage and high promotional input is over, so that firms remaining in the market often continue to make solid profits. Outstanding examples of old products remaining profitable include tobacco and certain ethical drugs which medical practitioners will still prescribe even though newer and more expensive products now dominate the market. The drug industry is nothing if not high value added and many of its old products will have gross manufacturers' margins of around 80–85 per cent (mark-ups of 400–567 per cent).

US cinema statistics provide us with a picture of a market in long-term decline which never quite expires. During the 1920s cinema admissions increased strongly to a peak in 1929

---

[6] Exchange arrangements exist for the transfer of 'time slots' between owners, to enable holders to savour the delights of another time-share location and yet another golf course.

Table 3 US average weekly cinema admissions for selected years (1921–70)

	millions
1921	27
1924	56
1929	110
1932	50
1941	55
1948	80
1949	70
1950	60
1960	44
1970	15

A key factor in many declining markets is that the occasional buyer will have dropped out, so that the market is effectively reconstituted of a harder base of buyers whose demand is stronger. This allows for the possibility of increasing prices, and the film industry has managed to do this, at the same time as introducing the multiplex ten-screen cinema and other innovations, which are drawing cinema-goers back to the movies.

The corporate history of MGM provides an outstanding example of a company written off by financial analysts in 1970 making its powerful presence felt in another field of entertainment. Metro-Goldwyn-Mayer, created as the result of a merger of studio production facilities, film distribution networks and a theatre chain in 1924, surely offered the best known set of all corporate initials. The severe decline in cinema admissions resulted in MGM showing an operating loss worldwide of $8.3m for 1970. However, the asset sell-off programme had yielded $9.8m, leaving a surplus of $1.5m for that year. By 1973, MGM had sold off most of its studio properties and all its overseas theatres and music companies.

It hired out to television, but did not sell, its film copyrights, and invested in two enormous resort hotels. The MGM Grand Hotel in Las Vegas, the world's largest resort hotel with 2084 rooms, opened in 1974 with bookings through to 1982. This was followed by the 1015-room MGM Grand at Reno, Nevada in 1978, which incorporated the world's largest casino.

All this plus the fact that Clark Gable as Rhett Butler, and Vivien Leigh, as Scarlett O'Hara, broke all-time US viewership records (110m in November 1976) with a showing of the 1939 classic *Gone with the Wind*. As an interesting sidelight on this, in 1937 David O. Selznick, having purchased the film rights from author Margaret Mitchell for $50,000, believed he had found something so outstanding that he voluntarily paid the author another $50,000. It is almost impossible to imagine a similar occurrence of commercial generosity today.

The financial results of the turnaround were revealed in the final accounts for the year 1976, showing net profits of $35.5m – an all-time high. By 1978 the net income statement disclosed profits exceeding $49m, and even the analysts were saying that the recovery was looking good.[7]

Eurotunnel

Simultaneously launched in London and Paris in November 1987, Eurotunnel carried the hallmarks of the definitive high-risk investment of the 1980s and beyond. It has a number of unique features worthy of enumeration. The twinning of shares and warrants enabled early investors taking the long view to make, so to speak, a through booking for the trip of a lifetime, by investing in the shares. Others, with possibly more speculative short-term interest, selected the new warrants, joining the train whenever it seemed to make an unscheduled stop due to cost over-runs, causing the shares and, hence, the warrants to fall back temporarily.

The warrants, exercisable between 15 November 1990 and 15 November 1992, expire six months before the tunnel is due to become operational in May 1993. Ten of the warrants plus approximately 460p (for UK resident investors) may be exchanged for one unit during their two-year life. For example, at the close of business on 22 February 1990, Eurotunnel units were trading at 595p, having fluctuated between 376p and 1172p during the previous twelve months. The warrants closed at 45p with a corresponding high/low of 90p/31p. The issue price of 350p per unit represented 1E(PLC) share, 1E(SA) share plus 1E(PLC) warrant and 1E(SA) warrant. Share units and twinned warrants were then separately traded. Both units and warrants seem to possess at least one of the basic requirements for the options market: that of volatility.

Investors in from the start at 350p would probably describe the experience in a word as unforgettable; one might also hope profitable. At the quoted price of 595p, deducting 460p for a hypothetical cost of conversion, on 15 November 1992, we have a balance of 135p/10 = 13 $\frac{1}{2}$p as an approximation of the intrinsic worth of the warrants. Since the warrants closed at 45p, the difference of 31 $\frac{1}{2}$p represents time value.

Whether such a proposition is attractive to an investor will be largely judgemental, although an investor making full use of the travel concession could enjoy it. The offer for sale included not only two official disclaimers

[7] *The MGM Story.* J. D. Eames, 1979.

but a reference to the fact that the projections did not constitute a forecast, as they would be materially affected by economic change! Investors' attention was also drawn to the point that the first payday was way out, since no dividend is now planned before 1999. This high-risk investment thus carries the international classification Certificate A (for adults only).

At first sight the projections have the stamp of an ambitious managing director's X per cent per year growth to infinity, as the original revenue projections implied an expected average annual compound increase over the period 1993–2041 of 27 per cent. Still, we should not be unduly pessimistic, as a number of long-range transport studies have in the past come up with substantial underestimates of traffic volumes. Perhaps Edison's[8] forecast in 1896, the year of the first public showing of a motion picture, of seventy-eight cinemas as the ultimate number for the whole of the US might have relevance as an example of a commercial misjudgement by an extremely sharp businessman. In the event, the number of cinemas reached 14,637 by 1926, when Hollywood was virtually at its peak.

Compilation of a series of unofficial journey times from information made available in the offer document and other sources, provisionally suggests an estimated rail journey time via the tunnel of 3 hours 45 minutes from London (City) EC2, to Paris Gare du Nord. This must give rail the inside track in any day-by-day London–Paris race against air travel via Heathrow–Orly, although on a nice day a short take-off service via London City Airport (Stolport) E16, to Paris Charles de Gaulle or Orly must have a timing advantage and probably a financial one for the user. It would remain, however, a much more weather-affected journey.

To awaken latent memories, Bradshaw of April 1959 timetabled the Golden Arrow, London (Victoria) to Paris (Nord) at 7 hours 40 minutes. A comparison of revised rail timings between the two capital cities of London and Paris is thus expected to show an unprecedented reduction over a period of thirty-five years of around 60 per cent for a 244-rail-mile journey.

In the offer document Eurotunnel divides its market into four main revenue sectors: passengers, passengers and vehicles, road freight and rail freight. This should give plenty of opportunity to introduce a range of differential tariffs aimed at maximizing utilization of tunnel capacity and to enable it to take full advantage of very profitable marginal revenues arising from a high fixed-cost base, to knock out competition from cross-channel ferries and airlines.

---

[8] Inventor of the kinetoscope (forerunner of the film camera), inventor of the incandescent electric lamp with Joseph Swan; also made improvements to the original stock ticker tape.

Finally, we might take a brief look at some of the socio-economic consequences of the tunnel. Could not Ashford, in Kent, become an inland freight and transit centre of a size to rival Chicago in the 1920s? And we should perhaps weigh up the possibilities of an enterprise zone or freeport in south-east Kent, which certainly looks on the cards.

Perhaps this may be the first draft of a TELEX in the style of the 1950s from a London agent updating his principal, a fictional Paris banker:

Addressee:	VP-LRP Banque Commerciale et Maritime SA, Paris
Ref:	All risks/FEW/WHA/145/332/LOND/SE/LEA295
Telegraphic address:	MARKERLOND
Dateline:	LONDON EIEI0
Time:	ZERO
Message reads:	CHUNNEL UK REGIONAL EFFECT SIGNIFICANT ANY TIME SCALE STOP WILL ADVISE SOONEST POSITION FERRIES/AIRLINE TARIFFS LOCATION EZONE/FREEPORT STOP FAIRFAX

5. Stock Market Information and Networks

Information is to markets as petroleum and gas oil are to transportation systems: this is not an overstatement. We must of course distinguish information from propaganda, which Lord Northcliffe defined as 'any systematic attempt to influence the public mind in a given direction'.

In all fields the use of coded expressions has become more widespread, and their interpretation something of a cult. Most examples are too well known to need further amplification, although we might mention the banker's, 'good for your figure, in a series'; the headmaster's, 'a good worker, but in need of a certain amount of supervision'; the sportsman's, 'we were perhaps a little too strong for them'. One misses sometimes the uncompromising tone of the old newsreels such as, 'Intelligence reports suggest opposing forces digging in for the winter. None the less the advance continues in extremely difficult terrain . . .'

There are so many different ways of saying the same thing. Some people like to infer, others to make their message clear. Here are a few managerial phrases with their more direct alternatives:

'This situation may require some attention': 'Go in swinging the axe'
'All our revenue budgets show positive variances': 'We are making tons of money'
'We are looking into the question of morale': 'People dislike coming to work here!'

Networks; sources and databases

Commercial and other large organizations have long had extensive intelligence networks, some worldwide, combined with immensely detailed databases. Examples include banking, the Inland Revenue, HM

Customs, the police via Interpol and Scotland Yard's National Criminal Intelligence Service (NCIS), shipping agents and charterers, and bookmakers' wire and satellite information services. Informal managerial networks are also in existence in the UK, including the exchange of information in personnel matters, industry economics and the pooling of regional sales data via independent third parties to monitor short-term trade swings.

In a book whose title implies the instant product it would be unwise to suggest that investors follow this or that newspaper's City comment,[1] buy this or that financial journal, subscribe to this or that stock market newsletter, or use a particular bank or broker, since the International Stock Exchange, London EC2, will supply a list of brokers undertaking private client work. It is assumed that all this is known, and that an investor whose general intentions are first to make an intellectual assessment of data rather than to act instinctively on the latest buzz or rumour, will have such things in hand.

However, something ought perhaps to be said on the question of reference material in general, and must be said on the matter of more specialized financial databases in particular. In the matter of general reference sources we might expect Sherlock Holmes to have taken *Bradshaw's Railway Guide* (first published in 1839), and *Bartholomew's Gazetteer of the British Isles*, the first edition of which dates from 1887. We would expect the man of some means and connoisseur of crime to have the definitive eighty-three-volume set of Hodge's *Notable British Trials*, the general medical practitioner to have *MIMS*, and the motor trader *Glass's Guide*.

At this point the interests of the Inland Revenue in dividends and capital gains tax should be mentioned. All Inland Revenue offices subscribe to the Extel UK Capital Gains Tax Service, to the annual Dividend and Interest Record and other investor tabulations, which provide valuable checks on financial information made available by individual taxpayers.

A stockbroker would have both the *Daily Official List*[2] of prices and the *Weekly Official Intelligence*,[3] *Who's Who* and Whittaker, also the *Stock Exchange Year Book*, a definitive source of information on listed companies, again available in the reference section of large public libraries. He would

---

[1] Following the crash of 1825, newspapers began to publish daily accounts of Stock Exchange dealings and security prices for the first time.
[2] Published daily since 1843.
[3] Dating from 1882. Its forerunner, *The Railway Intelligence* dates from 1839 and *Bradshaw's Railway Almanack, Directory and Shareholders Guide* would appear to date from 1848 and continued publication until 1923.

also have Dun and Bradstreet's *Top 50,000 UK Companies*. All stockbrokers subscribe to the Extel Card Service for 2900 UK listed companies; the full service with daily update costs £3510 (January 1991), an increase since 1970 (£440) roughly in line with inflation, and many to the analyst's service and Extel taxation service. Other services the specialist stockbroker might use include *Crawford's City Connections*, the *Directory of Directors*, Macmillan's *Unquoted Companies*. These are all expensive publications available in the largest libraries.

Private investors seeking an individual company card for their own reference (these are available in many large libraries of major cities, but photocopying of them is not allowed) pay £16 for information on each company, against the equivalent of 12 ½p in 1970, an increase of 12,700 per cent, or seventeen times the 1970 cost in real terms after having cancelled out the effect of inflation. A cheaper alternative may be to write to the secretary's office of a company in which the investor may be interested, asking for a copy of the latest report and accounts, which will show, among other things, a five-year run back of financial results. Accounts of very large concerns are also often available in the reference sections of large libraries.

The Extel card – important to the private investor, vital to the professional – includes the following company information on the main card:

- date of registration
- address of registered office
- objects of the company
- directors
- capital structure
- details of capitalization issues
- dividend declaration dates, payment dates and dates *ex div*
- net amounts per share
- for certain companies net assets per share are shown
- high/low for the shares over the past ten years
- profit and loss accounts and balance sheet summaries for the last five years

The yellow updating card includes:

- earnings yields
- dividend yields
- PE ratios for a range of hypothetical share price levels

- summary of recent dividend payments
- interim results
- announcements or events affecting the company

For more specialized users, such as stockbrokers, as mentioned earlier, Extel offer the analyst's service (blue cards), USM service, overseas service and the monthly new issues and placings service. Other specialized services include Extel or McCarthy's on-line computerized company service and McCarthy's card service (pink cards). Extel on-line service for individual cards costs £1 per minute plus 4p per line (January 1991). Stockbrokers might also subscribe to any one of a number of chart services for evaluation of the technical position.

At first sight an Extel company card is a daunting prospect. It would not be appropriate in an introductory work of this nature to give examples of calculations based on the cards as these are dealt with elsewhere.[4] However, to assist those unfamiliar with Extel cards or the on-line services, try this seven-point plan:

1. Check year end.
2. Check dividend dates, *ex div* dates and dividend amounts.
3. Verify market capitalization (number of shares issued × price) – *The Times* has market capitalization figures on Monday in its easy to read, alphabetical, sector by sector share classification, starting with banks and finishing with water.
4. Check PE against sector average in *Financial Times* under FT-Actuaries Index. Check yield against sector and all industrial yields.
5. Look at large holdings.
6. Check net assets per share – work it out if not tabulated.
7. Review and then read on at leisure.

Other sources of information available to inner circle City investors and brokers include visits to companies and briefings, the results of which are often subsequently made public. These latter are given on any one of three levels:

Off the Record: Confidential, no disclosure allowed in any circumstances
On the Record: Information and source may be quoted

---

[4] *Investing in the Stock Market.* E. B. Groves, 1987.

Backgrounder: Information made available may be quoted, the source remaining undisclosed. The standard formula for the backgrounder is 'Sources close to the company suggest . . .'

Essential calculations

In terms of dealing expenses, the odds have moved in favour of the private investor since Big Bang. Before then, the average spread (difference between bid and offer prices) for widely traded stocks, was around 3 per cent, with transfer stamp at 1 per cent, broker's commission, taking a £10,000 transaction, 1.65 per cent on the first £7000 and 1.25 per cent on the remaining £3000 (an average of 1.53 per cent on £10,000 value plus VAT at 15 per cent).

The contract note in Figure 6 shows a purchase of 10,000 LASMO at 130p on 8 September 1986 (just before Big Bang) at a total buying cost on a consideration of £13,000 to be £349.67.

At Big Bang transfer stamp came down to 0.5 per cent. Spreads on alpha stocks were reduced to about 1 per cent. In the case of a widely traded international stock like Hanson, closing prices in *The Times* of Friday, 23 February 1990 were 219 ½p (bid) 220p (offer), a spread of less than 0.25 per cent. Further, on 1 January 1990, brokers' commission became exempt from VAT. This is shown on the contract note in Figure 7, in respect of the purchase of 10,000 Eurotunnel warrants at 47p on 19 February 1990. The remaining 0.5 per cent transfer duty is expected to be removed in the short term,[5] to equalize costs of transacting business in London with those of other major international centres. Note also the commission terms for the transaction-only service on the Eurotunnel Contract Note.

To summarize the present position, an investor buying through a broker on a typical transaction-only service tariff 5000 shares at 100p on 8 February 1990 would receive a contract note incorporating the following:

```
Bought for your account 5000 KDM at 100p =   £5000.00
Transfer stamp (½ per cent)     £25.00
Brokerage (1 per cent)           50.00
                                 ─────
                                               75.00
                                             ────────
                                             £5075.00
```

---

[5] The 1990 Budget announced the removal of the 0.5 per cent stamp duty on share transactions, to coincide with the introduction of the TAURUS system.

Williams de Broë

Williams de Broë Hill Chaplin & Company Limited
P.O. Box 515, Pinners Hall
Austin Friars, London EC2P 2HS

And Stock Exchange

STOCKBROKERS

TELEPHONES: OFFICE 01-588 7511 DEALING BOX: 01-588 16445

TELEX 893277
FACSIMILE 01-588 1702

CONTRACT NOTE

REGISTERED NO. 983271 ENGLAND
VAT REGISTRATION NO. 243 7861 45

BARCLAYS BANK PLC

BOUGHT FOR YOUR ACCOUNT   389

CLIENT NUMBER	BARGAIN NUMBER	BARGAIN DATE	SETTLEMENT
BARCL0042	QNB116	26 AUG 1986	08 SEP 1986

QUANTITY	TITLE	PRICE	CONSIDERATION (N)	TRANSFER STAMP (N)	CONT STAMP (N)	P.T.M LEVY (N)	OTHER CHARGES	(T) or (E)	COMMISSION (T)	VAT @ 15 %	TOTAL
10000	LONDON & SCOTTISH MARINE OIL ORD 25P	130P	13000.00	130.00 (1%)	0.00	0.60			190.50*	28.57	£13349.67
	TO531696										
	7000.00 @ 1.65%*6000.00 @ 1.25%*								SHARE 25%	(UNDER APPENDIX 41)	263

COMMISSION RATE

THE MANAGER
BARCLAYS BANK PLC

For and on behalf of
WILLIAMS de BROE HILL CHAPLIN & COMPANY LIMITED

SUBJECT TO THE RULES AND REGULATIONS OF THE STOCK EXCHANGE

MEMBER OF THE STOCK EXCHANGE
In view of Capital Gains Tax all Contracts and Statements should be retained.

E. & O.E.

VAT SYMBOLS: (T) = TAXABLE (E) = EXEMPT (N) = OUTSIDE THE SCOPE * = COMMISSION DIVISIBLE WITH YOURSELVES

REF. C01/1

Figure 6, LASMO contract note

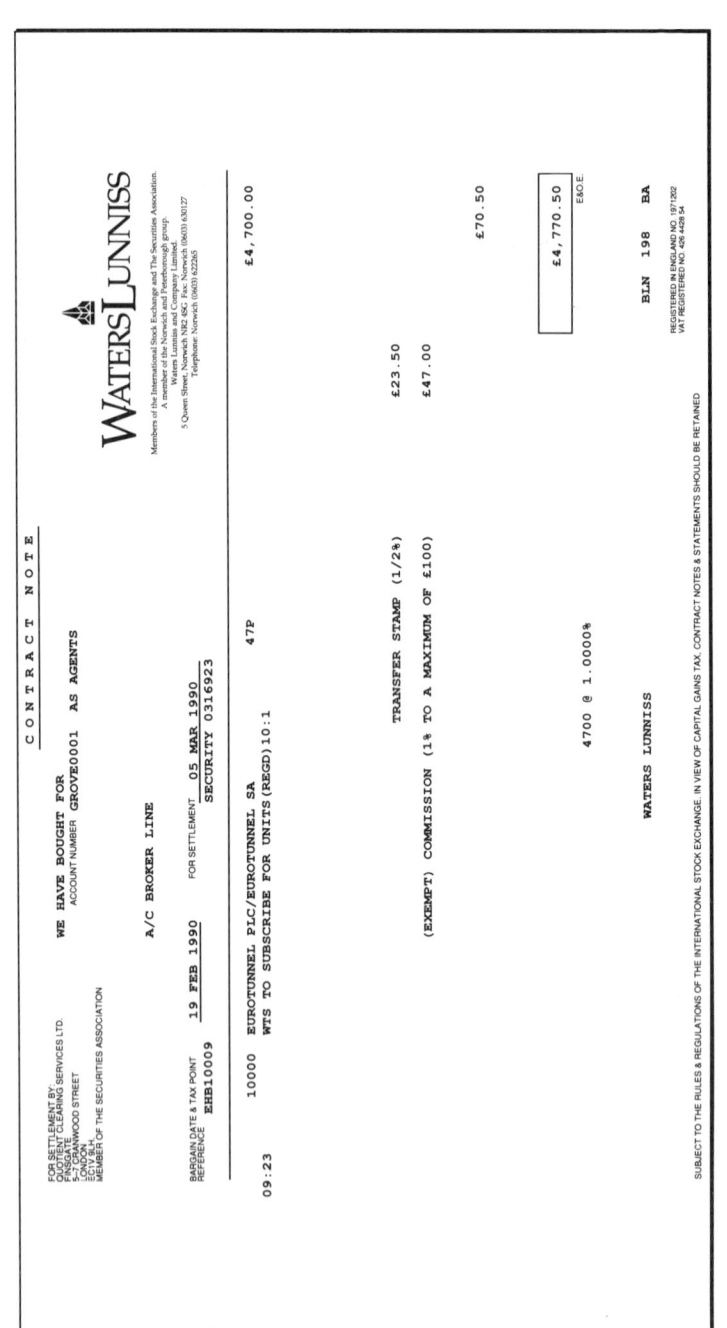

```
                                                CONTRACT  NOTE

FOR SETTLEMENT BY                    WE HAVE BOUGHT FOR
QUOTIENT CLEARING SERVICES LTD.      ACCOUNT NUMBER GROVE0001    AS AGENTS
FINSGATE
5-7 CRANWOOD STREET
LONDON
EC1V 9LH
MEMBER OF THE SECURITIES ASSOCIATION
                                                                                    ▲
                                     A/C BROKER LINE                          WATERSLUNNISS
                                                                   Members of the International Stock Exchange and The Securities Association.
                                                                             A member of the Norwich and Peterborough group.
                                                                                   Waters Lunniss and Company Limited.
BARGAIN DATE & TAX POINT  19 FEB 1990    FOR SETTLEMENT  05 MAR 1990         5 Queen Street, Norwich NR2 4SF. Fax: Norwich (0603) 630127
REFERENCE     EHB10009                         SECURITY 0316923                        Telephone: Norwich (0603) 622265

09:23    10000   EUROTUNNEL PLC/EUROTUNNEL SA                 47P                             £4,700.00
                 WTS TO SUBSCRIBE FOR UNITS (REGD)10:1


                                              TRANSFER STAMP (1/2%)        £23.50
                 (EXEMPT) COMMISSION (1% TO A MAXIMUM OF £100)             £47.00
                                                                                                £70.50


                                            4700 @ 1.0000%

                                                                                              £4,770.50
                                          WATERS LUNNISS                                         E.&O.E.

                                                                                     BLN  198   BA

                                                                                REGISTERED IN ENGLAND NO. 1971202
                                                                                VAT REGISTERED NO. 436 4428 54

  SUBJECT TO THE RULES & REGULATIONS OF THE INTERNATIONAL STOCK EXCHANGE. IN VIEW OF CAPITAL GAINS TAX, CONTRACT NOTES & STATEMENTS SHOULD BE RETAINED
```

Figure 7, Eurotunnel contract note

The settlement date is 19 February, which means the buyer's cheque has to be in the broker's hands at the start of business that day. Contract levy is ignored.

A direct comparison with Figure 6 covering the purchase of LASMO at 130p on 26 August 1986, shows expenses, excluding PTM levy,[6] of £349.07. Using the above transaction-only basis and assuming LASMO traded at 130p on 19 February 1990, expenses would be:

Stamp duty (0.5 per cent)	£65.00
Brokerage/commission (1 per cent), subject to a maximum of	£100.00
	£165.00

This is a reduction of almost 50 per cent on the August 1986 charge, leaving aside the advantage of narrower dealing margins.

Dealing via bank or broker made no difference to small and middle investors at that time. However, commission scales for transactions put through banks now differ from brokers' charges (see Chapter Two for commission scales).[7] Of course, many investors, quite understandably, prefer to deal with their broker on the pre-Big Bang full service basis, paying higher commission for receiving general financial advice.

The dividend yield on a share is simply the gross dividend expressed as a percentage of the current share price. For example, if FWS Motors is at 145p on 3 January 1990 and has declared a net total annual dividend of $4\frac{1}{2}$p, the gross yield is determined by adding back to the net dividend the 25 per cent tax deducted before the dividend warrants are despatched to shareholders, i.e. $4\frac{1}{2}p \times 100/75 = 6p$ gross dividend. Hence, $6 \times 100/145$ = 4.1 per cent gross yield.

We should also perhaps touch on the concept of growth yield. This occurs where an investor receives an increasing return on his investment, which may arise in three ways:

1. Increasing dividends, but no increase in share price
2. Increase in share price, but dividends unchanged or no dividends paid
3. Increase in share price consequent upon progressive increases in profits and dividends

This third category of share is the growth stock par excellence.

---

[6] PTM (Panel for Takeovers and Mergers) levy of £2 on transactions of £5000+, with effect from 1 April 1991.
[7] Investors should realize that since Big Bang dealing expenses have been subject to numerous adjustments.

The concept of the price earnings (PE) ratio or multiple is North American in origin and is simply a convenient shorthand way of saying that such and such a share is worth so many years' earnings at current levels. If LGW Aggregates is trading at 260p, paying net dividends of 18p out of earnings of 28; the PE becomes 260/28 = 9.3. The share price represents 9.3 × the latest earnings per share or the share sells for 9.3 × annual earnings. Thus, P/e = m(multiple) or P = me. We need not be mesmerized by this, but the idea arrived on the London Market in the early 1960s following the introduction in 1962 of the new FT-Actuaries Index, which gave an alphabetical sub-classification of thirty-four industrial sectors from building materials to water, oil and gas, plus nine financial sectors.

The availability of this composite index immediately facilitated all the necessary statistical comparisons for price earnings ratios, covers, yields, and incorporated an *ex div* adjustment, all of which were sadly lacking in the FT-30 Index. For each individual share it is now possible to make the following significant comparisons:

1. Share v. Sector, i.e. building share v. building sector average.
2. Share v. Share within sector.
3. Share v. All Industrial (479 share) Index.
4. Share v. Time – a comparison over time of PE, dividend yield, cover, etc.
5. Sector v. Sector.

In other words, this index tabulation allows analysis backwards, forwards, sideways and diagonally *ad infinitum*. For practical purposes the instant investor would make most use of comparisons 1 and 3.

On the subject of PE ratios in general, these can be valuable to individual investors as a gauge of the market's 'barometric pressure'. For example, in October 1929, when the US market collapsed, on the basis of available statistics the PE multiple at the peak (for US stocks) in July 1929 was around 20. In mid-1973 the UK market peaked at around a multiple of 22. In October 1987 the UK figure was just 19 when the safety valve blew. On 3 January 1990, the PE for the FT- Actuaries All Industrial (479 share) Index was 12.39; by 7 December 1990 it was 10.50. Need anything more be said?

A moving average is one of the simplest trends. In the case of certain stock market series of share prices and indices of market average, the seasonal element may be conveniently considered as part of the short-term irregular movement. Take the example of an economic time series representing period data, such as monthly deliveries into consumption of cement. The seasonal element will consist of a two-stage adjustment – first, for differences in the number of working days in each calendar month and second, an adjustment for true and significant residual seasonal movement, which regularly occurs between, say, January and July, in the sales of many products including cement, bricks, oil for central heating, soft drinks, ice cream and so on.

For stock market series, seasonal represents values at specified times (point data), hence, obviously, no calendar adjustment is necessary for variations in lengths of months. Although some industrial sectors will be regularly weather affected, such as building and catering, all shares will as a generalization move in anticipation of their interim and final reporting dates and dividend announcements. Further, most shares respond to Budget expectations, surprise events and interest rate changes. Thus seasonal and irregular (random) fluctuations are for practical forecasting purposes usefully combined in any statistical analysis of short-term share price movements.

A moving average of daily closing share prices or index values smooths out the seasonal and irregular (SI) movements, leaving a trend and cycle (TC) indicator.[8] Generally, the length of the moving average is then selected to correspond with the period of the short-term cycle: fourteen months, thirteen weeks, two-hundred days, fifty days, twenty days are typical lengths. Technically, an even period moving average needs centring where the twelve-month moving average is adjusted to align with July (month seven) instead of lying between June and July. This is achieved by summing the moving annual total (MAT) in pairs, and then dividing by 24. It is important for the chart investor to realize that the longer the moving average cycle, the more sluggish it will be in reflecting changes in the series. Consider, for example, a fifty-day average of the FT-SE 100 Index of closing prices, showing 1850 for Day 1 closing; 1783 at the close of business on Day 50. Day 51 (actual) is recorded as 1813 against Day 50 (actual) of 1783, i.e. +30 points. Hence, the actual series of the FT-SE 100 (closing prices) will move up on Day 51, although the corresponding moving average turns down slightly, because Day 51, coming into the series at 1813, displaces Day 1, dropping out, with a value of 1850, i.e. −37 points.

A full explanation of moving averages will be found in a variety of text-books on statistical method or business statistics.

---

[8] An examination of a financial series will usually indicate the average distance between peaks, and hence an approximation of the duration of the short-term cycle.

Of shares and shareholders

Buying in shares

A company may purchase its own shares for cancellation under section 46 of the Companies Act 1981. Where shares are at a discount to net assets, this can be advantageous to the remaining shareholders. For example, a company whose shares are trading at 100p, with recent valuation of net assets per share of 110p, is in effect cancelling a potential claim to 110p by the payment of £1.

A further example shows another aspect: a company wishes to redeem some of its ordinary shares, with £1m earning interest net of 10 per cent, after payment of 35 per cent corporation tax,[9] with earnings per share (EPS) of 16p and its shares currently trading at 160p. Now, it follows that £1m could redeem 625,000 shares at 160p; since interest of £100,000/16p (EPS) = 625,000. In fact, at a price of 160p the redemption of 625,000 shares means the company has traded interest received for equivalent corporate earnings. Obviously, the number of shares redeemed without any dilution of EPS, will always depend on the relationship between the three factors: net interest, share price and EPS. Dilution of earnings will not occur where shares are redeemed from reserves.

Scrip issues

A scrip issue is a free bonus issue of shares to an existing class of shareholder. As the company receives no consideration for the shares its net worth is unchanged. The price of the shares will fall in proportion to the increase in the number of shares. In other words, share price and quantity are in reciprocal relationship. Thus a scrip issue of one for one means the number of shares is increased by $2/1 \times$ (price) $^1\!/_2 = 1$, so the overall value is unchanged. To amplify this, consider this example: Company A announced a one for three scrip issue with its share price standing at 176p. Other things remaining unchanged the ex-scrip price will be: $^3\!/_4 \times 176p = 132p$ XC. To check we note that $4 \times 132p$ XC $= 3 \times 176p = 528p$.

Scrip dividends

Mention must now be made of the procedure whereby a company capitalizes its dividend payment. Such arrangements were commonplace in the US in the roaring twenties and gained considerable notoriety. Some US

---

[9] For 1991/92 the standard rate of corporation tax was reduced to 33 per cent by the 1991 Budget.

companies paid so-called stock dividends over a number of years, including dividends paid in shares of subsidiaries: spin-offs. Shareholders never received any actual cash, but presumably were satisfied by surging prices until the 1929 collapse. In effect, the stock or scrip dividend means that shareholders are increasing their risk capital each time they accept stock in lieu of dividend, and the company retains more cash and defers advance corporation tax (ACT). Companies unable to make a full recovery of ACT will find the stock dividend even more attractive, as non-recoverable ACT is eliminated. Stock dividends are taxable in the hands of higher rate taxpayers in the UK. Holders of bearer shares must convert to registered form before they can receive scrip dividends. A standard form of election for shareholders to receive scrip dividends in lieu of cash is illustrated in Figure 8.

Rights issues

A rights issue is a proportionate offer of shares at a discount to existing shareholders. It is used where a company requires funds for expansion, but does not wish to increase its gearing via loan stock or debentures. As with most investments, shareholders subscribe to the rights issue as an act of faith, and often on the implied assumption that the existing rate of dividend will be paid on the enlarged capital. In the event of shareholder disappointment, the damage to the share price could be considerable.

Under this procedure, all shareholders receive a provisional letter of allotment. The shares are dealt in ex rights (XR) when the letters of allotment have reached members. Shareholders who do not wish to take up the rights may sell the allotment letter representing the value of their rights. These have been subject to stamp duty from March 1986, if anyone but the original holder is registered as a shareholder. A sale of rights will place them in the equivalent financial position to shareholders subscribing to the issue. The rights issue, unlike the scrip issue, brings money into the company, and thereby increases its assets. The investor needs to know both the value of the rights (nil paid) as represented by the letter of allotment and the share price XR, when shareholders have received their allotment letter. Consider an example: A company whose shares stand at 100p announces a rights issue of one for four at 80p.

$$\text{Price XR} = 4 \times 100p + 1 \times 80p = 480p/5 = 96p \text{ XR}$$

Hence price ex rights:	96p
Cost of rights:	80p
Nil paid value =	16p

Box 1
Name and Address of Holder

Registered Office:

London EC2
(Registered in England No. 103002)

Box 2 Number of ordinary shares registered in your name at close of business on 10th February 1989	Box 3 Maximum number of ordinary shares in respect of which an election can be made.	Box 4 Number of new ordinary shares to be allotted in respect of the maximum election entitlement shown in Box 3.	Box 5 *Number of new ordinary shares you wish to receive if less than in Box 4.

*Only complete Box 5 if you wish to receive a lesser number of new ordinary shares than your maximum entitlement shown in Box 4. If no number or a number in excess of your entitlement is inserted, this form will be treated as an election to receive the number of shares shown in Box 4.

FORM OF ELECTION
Fully paid ordinary shares instead of cash in respect of the final dividend for the year ended 30th September 1988

If you wish to receive the final dividend and the first interim dividend IN CASH on the whole of your holding of ordinary shares you should NOT complete this Form of Election.

If you wish to receive new ordinary shares of the Company, credited as fully paid, instead of cash in respect of all or part of your holding you must complete and sign this Form and return it, folded as indicated on the reverse, to the Company's registrars, National Westminster Bank PLC, Registrar's Department, P.O. Box No. 82, Caxton House, Redcliffe Way, Bristol BS99 7YA, so as to arrive by close of business on **10th March 1989**. UNLESS THIS IS DONE YOU WILL RECEIVE THE DIVIDENDS IN CASH ON THE WHOLE OF YOUR HOLDING.

Box 4 shows your maximum entitlement to new shares. You may elect to receive any lesser number by completing Box 5.

To the Directors of .... ("the Company"):-

I/We the undersigned being the registered holder(s) at the close of business on 10th February 1989 of ordinary shares in the Company hereby irrevocably elect, subject to fulfilment of the conditions set out below, to receive an allotment of the number of new ordinary shares shown in Box 4 above (or, if less, the number shown in Box 5 above), credited as fully paid, on the terms of the letter from the Company dated 16th February 1989 and the Memorandum and Articles of Association of the Company as from time to time varied, instead of the final dividend for the year ended 30th September 1988 of 8p per ordinary share and the first interim dividend for the year ending 30th September 1989 of 3p per ordinary share. I/We agree that this election is subject to the following conditions: the middle market quotation for the Company's ordinary shares as derived from the Daily Official List on 10th March 1989 being not less than 296p; the passing of Resolution No. 11 at the 1989 Annual General Meeting† of the Company; and the admission of the new ordinary shares to the Official List by the Council of The International Stock Exchange.

I/We hereby authorise you to send at my/our risk by first class post a definitive share certificate in respect of any new ordinary shares allotted to me/us pursuant to this Form of Election.

Dated 1989

(1) Signature ....

Address to which Certificate is to be sent
(if different from registered address shown above).

BLOCK CAPITALS ....

....

....

(2) Signature ....

(3) Signature ....

(4) Signature ....

....
In the case of joint holders ALL must sign. In the case of a corporation this form should be executed under its common seal or be signed by a duly authorised official whose capacity should be stated.

Figure 8, Standard form of election for scrip dividends

A logical check on the blended (weighted) average calculation shows that the investor taking up the rights pays 80p and ends up with five shares at 96p for every four originally held. His net value prior to payment is thus 5 × 96p − 80p = 400p. The investor who declines the offer finds himself with four shares at 96p plus an allotment letter worth 16p = 4 × 96p + 16p = 400p and so is in the equivalent position of the shareholder taking up the offer.

New issues, including privatizations

Prospectuses of new issues always make them sound attractive. Share application forms appear frequently in newspapers such as the *Daily Telegraph*, *The Times* and the *Financial Times*. Certain new issues may have a lot going for them as long as investors realize that they are often paying many times more than the directors of the firm offering the shares. New investors are always taking most of the risk, and, if the issue is heavily over-subscribed, applicants may end up with an offer of fewer shares than they originally applied for, or no allocation at all, for a fair amount of inconvenience.

There are, of course, numerous examples of major new privatization issues which have been successful in recent years, including Telecom, TSB, British Gas, and the water and electricity companies.

Water privatization: Here is an example of dividend yields, for investors taking advantage of the privatization offer, of two of the water companies privatized in December 1989:

	Welsh Water	Northumbrian Water
	%	%
Year 1 (December 1989–October 1990)	15.96	15.27
Year 2	13.14	12.57
Year 3	10.15	9.71
Average of three years:	13.08	12.52

Notes:

1. Dividends for year one are annualized payments of the final dividend for year ended 31 March 1990, paid in October 1990.
2. Yield calculations assume a minimum holding of 1500 shares and that the investor elects to take the share discount offers.

For the yield and resource investor, the financial inducement was undeniable and the issue was soon showing substantial capital appreciation: in fact, an all winners programme.

Electricity privatization: The electricity offer of November 1990 was, like the earlier water issues, heavily oversubscribed. The fact that the private investor was patronized by 'user friendly' publicity, below the lowest intellectual level, did not appear to worry the five million plus applicants representing over twelve million applications for shares in the twelve distribution companies covering England and Wales. On the first day of trading the shares of all regional electricity companies went to a substantial premium in their 100p partly paid form, the highest being Manweb, touching 178p. Some aspects of the launch timetable may eventually be of historical interest, as in an unprecedented arrangement it allowed the underwriters to withdraw the issue in the following circumstances:

a) an outbreak of hostilities in the Persian Gulf between the issue of the prospectus on 26 November and midnight on Monday 10 December 1990, the day of the announcement of share allocations.
b) Bank of England agreement that an outbreak of hostilities would cause a fall in London share prices.
c) the underwriters reasonably believed that electricity shares would be trading at a discount by the close of business on the first day of dealing, Tuesday 11 December.

A worked example of the yield in years one and two, i.e. 1991–2 for a registered customer allocated 100 shares in Merseyside and North Wales Electricity Board (MANWEB):

Calendar year 1991 (Year 1)   £
Initial application December 1990: 100 × £1   =   100
First instalment (22 October 1991): 100 × 70p   =   70
                                                  170

Dividend payable October 1991:
    11.20p net
    3.73p tax credit (25 per cent)
    14.93p × 100   =   14.93
Vouchers (1 August 1991):   £18.00
Grossed up for basic rate tax (25 per cent)   6.00
                                                  24.00
                                                  38.93

Effective gross yield – Year 1 = $\frac{38.93}{170} \times 100$ = 22.9 per cent

Calendar year 1992 (Year 2)   £
Amounts paid on application and first
  instalment in respect of 100 shares   =   170
Second instalment (15 September 1992): 70p × 100   =   70
                                                       ———
                                                       240
Expected dividends payable year ending 31 December 1992:
    16.00p net
    <u>5.33p</u> tax credit (25 per cent)
    21.33p × 100   = 21.33
Estimated effective gross yield − Year 2 = 8.89 per cent
Vouchers: nil

Notes:
1. Registered consumers choosing the voucher alternative will be subject to capital gains tax (CGT) on the net value of the vouchers, i.e. £18, where taxable gain exceeds the personal exemption limit of £5000 in the year of disposal.
2. Registered consumers choosing the bonus share alternative will be entitled to a one for ten share bonus of fully paid shares if their original holding is retained until 31 December 1993. For CGT purposes the value of the bonus shares will be taken as the closing price on 31 December 1993.
3. Cash dividend yields vary from 8.03 per cent for Eastern and Southern Electricity to 9.03 per cent for Northern Electricity.
4. The number of shares issued was 2157m, with a capital value of £5177m, of which private investors were allocated 50.6 per cent.
5. Timing of payment of the first and second instalments has been ignored in calculating gross yield.
6. Since the issue was ten times oversubscribed, approximately £26bn was effectively withdrawn from the public during the vital pre-Christmas period for the retail trade. The public was out of funds in respect of about £23bn from 4 December to (effectively) 28 December. At about 0.75 per cent net interest, this represented a pick-up for the banking system of around £170m. A stockbroker with a typical level of 100 bargains a day would have handled around 40,000 electricity share sales on the first dealing day: Tuesday 11 December 1990.

Electricity generating companies privatization: Under the terms of the offer, HM government made available to investors, at home and overseas, 60 per cent of the ordinary share capital of National Power and Powergen. The approximate number of shares issued were: National Power 764.8m, Powergen 468.8m, at a price of 175p for each share, of which 100p was payable on application by 6 March 1991 and the final 75p payable by 4 February 1992.

At this stage the investing public fully understood the short-term profit potential of these offers, if they had not entirely grasped the underlying fiscal logic for them. At the end of the first day of trading (12 March 1991), the shares of both National Power and Powergen closed at 138p in their partly paid form, thus yielding a nice profit to investors who had been required to apply for the shares as a package, i.e. the minimum application consisted of 186 National Power plus 114 Powergen, making 300 shares in total. Sale of the shares allowed the investor the option of selling both or either allocation or retaining both.

Turning to the underlying reasons for these 'sales of the century', HM government knows what most of the public are blissfully unaware of, namely that Great Britain, the world's first and therefore oldest industrial economy is in the last furlong of its 200-year run since 1815 and is struggling to maintain its current position.

Returning to the privatization of the generating companies, Joe and Jane Public certainly enjoyed themselves and were gaining in investment knowledge with every sell-off. So much so that one heard some such shareholders describing themselves as 'investors'. Although technically such a pronouncement could not be denied, the qualifications for an investor are, as we have seen, slightly more demanding than the simple application for and disposal of shares in a privatization issue.

Mental attitudes – hints for the new investor

An investor is not usually a Sherlock Holmes whose calm, logical judgement classified investigations as one, two or three pipe problems. The true investor lives on the edge of his seat with excitement and sometimes anxiety. If things go badly – and they often do – he bites the bullet and says little, hoping for better times and muttering to himself that price and value are by no means the same thing. If things are going well, it is difficult not to be buoyant, which is usually noticed by one's friends: rather like the golfer who says, 'One good shot I'm laughing, two I give a lesson.'

There is much in the late Maxwell Joseph's philosophy. Grand Metropolitan Hotels shares once languished at 19p during the 1974–5 crash. His view was, 'Leave a bit in for the other fellow,' that is, take a bit of profit now and then and never gloat over a great success; a casual comment is sufficient. After all, there is only one thing worse than a bad loser and that is a gloating winner. Any investor worthy of the description must be able to take it on the chin and realize that he bought the bad share, nobody made him.

Experienced investors know and others should understand that there are three price zones through which every share is continually passing: Zone A: cheap share, often dangerously cheap; Zone B: reasonable value; Zone C: expensive.

Ex div quotation

It is essential for the investor to have a clear understanding of the meaning of the XD quotation. Shares go *ex div* at the start of a trading account, and when it is first quoted *ex div* it will, other things remaining unchanged, fall by the net dividend amount. When a dividend is declared, a company closes its share register to allow compilation of the list of shareholders entitled to the dividend.

A typical timetable of events following an announcement of a dividend on 12 January 1990 would be:

Shares listed *ex div*:	5 February (Monday)
Date of record, for dividend payment purposes, or date when share register re-opened for registration of transfers:	16 February
Dividend paid:	2 April

The dividend would be paid on 2 April to shareholders on the register at 16 February. Any sale occurring between 5 February and 2 April is an *ex div* bargain; with the seller retaining the right to the dividend. Some newspapers mark the shares *ex div* from 5 February until 2 April; others from 5 February until 16 February (the date of record). Not all brokers' contract notes indicate an *ex div* sale or purchase. If you are uncertain, check.

Special trades

Before dealing in any of the following categories of shares, brokers have to apply to the quotations department of the ISE.

ISE Rule Number	*Classification of Special List Trades*
534 4(a)	Bargains marked in securities where principal market is outside UK and Republic of Ireland.

535 (2)	Bargains marked in securities not listed on any exchange.
535 (3)	Bargains marked for approved companies engaged solely in mineral exploration.

Capital Gains Tax (CGT)

A brief outline of this tax, which has been much simplified recently, may prove useful to the investor.

Capital gains tax in its present form was introduced in 1965–6, with short- and long-term gains separately treated. This provision has now been swept away. The individual position for 1991–2, as it applies to stockmarket investments, may be summarized as follows:

- Gains of up to £5500 in each tax year are exempt; above the exemption level gains are taxable at 25 per cent or 40 per cent.
- Gains in excess of exemption limit are added to income to determine marginal rate of tax.
- Husband and wife each have a separate exemption allowance.
- Buying and selling expenses are allowable for CGT purposes.
- Cost of shares may be indexed for inflation after March 1982.
- For shares purchased before 6 April 1982 and sold after 5 April 1985, indexation is calculated by reference to the higher of 31 March 1982 value or actual cost. Indexation of losses is now permitted. Losses must be used to offset subsequent gains *before* taking advantage of the annual exemption allowance.
- In the event of a part sale of a holding, the buying prices are averaged.
- CGT was abolished on government stocks and corporate bonds from 2 July 1986.
- CGT is payable on 1 December after the close of the tax year in which liability arises.

Towards the end of a tax year an investor may be showing an unrealized loss on one or two potentially promising shares, while having a CGT liability above the current exemption limit on realized profits. In these circumstances it can pay to 'bed and breakfast' the loss-makers, i.e. sell them to establish the loss and repurchase the next day in the same Stock Exchange account, which reduces the tax bill for the year. In circumstances where there have been no sales during a tax year, the investor may also wish to sell and repurchase up to the amount of the exemption limit, thus raising the base for future gains tax by using the exemption allowance before the tax year closes.

There are a number of inexpensive publications illustrating the workings of income tax and capital gains tax as they affect private individuals, but it may be of interest to note the precise effects of capital gains tax as it applies to profits from the sale of shares.

As has been said, capital gains are now added to income to determine the actual rate of tax payable. The nominal rates for 1991–2 are 25 per cent and 40 per cent, although the actual rate may vary within this range according to the taxpayer's income for the year including capital gains. The *actual* rate of capital gains tax payable will therefore be either 25 per cent, 40 per cent or any rate in between according to the balance of taxable gains falling within each tax band.

Investors should be careful to distinguish the nominal rates of direct taxation, i.e. those rates applicable by statute; the marginal rate, i.e. the highest rate payable by a UK resident taxpayer – 40 per cent in 1991–2; the average or effective rate of tax paid, i.e. actual tax paid expressed as a percentage of total income from all sources before tax; and the all-important rate of compliance. This latter rate will normally be applicable only to very large incomes of, say, £0.5m per annum and above, and can arise by means of expensive tax planning advice, so that a UK resident taxpayer with potentially an *average effective* liability of, say, 38.5 per cent is able to reduce it, perfectly legally, to an *actual* rate of, say, 20 per cent.[10]

Gains arising from options, warrants and futures are subject to gains tax. Profits from index betting are exempt.

Financial index numbers

Index numbers constitute a statistical means of measuring changes in a group of variables between two or more different time periods or points in time. For example, using the index of industrial production to compare output between calendar year 1984 and calendar year 1985, we should be making a comparison between two periods of time (period data). Looking at the FT-SE 100 Index for 3 January 1990 we note that at 10 a.m. on that day it registered 2457.2, whereas at 4 p.m. it registered 2463.7 – a comparison of two specific points in time (point data).

---

[10] Offshore trusts will in certain circumstances incur a liability for UK capital gains tax from Budget Day, 19 March 1991.

The weighting or use of factors proportionate to the relative importance of constituents in terms of value, quantity or price, the method of averaging, i.e. arithmetic, geometric, harmonic, whether fixed base or chain base, current weight or base weight, has fascinated economic statisticians for more than a century. As all the discussion turns on the significance of these technical factors, we may draw a veil over it for our purposes, except to mention that the matter is exhaustively treated in such works as *Index Numbers* by W. R. Crowe and Croxton & Cowden's *Applied General Statistics*, for those investors who may wish to pursue the matter.

What is of some interest, however, is the Retail Prices Index, a current weighted index as the constituents are updated every year, and a direct descendant of the Cost of Living Index devised by Professor A. L. Bowley in 1914 to measure changes in living costs of working-class families during World War I.

The Retail Prices Index has now become a universal bench mark of inflation in the UK, and for financial indexation purposes, though it suffers from certain weaknesses. Two examples will suffice:

1. Inclusion of mortgage interest at full cost when a deduction for the long-term investment element should be incorporated or estimated rental costs substituted.
2. No regional sub-indexes to reflect area variations in living costs.

Turning to financial indexes, we note their early use in America. The Dow Jones, an arithmetic unweighted average of thirty stocks, was first calculated in 1884. Of its eleven constituents at that time, nine were rails. During the 1890s, steels, tobacco, sugar and oil stocks were introduced to extend the number of items to twenty. The present base date for the Dow Jones Index – the world's best known stock market index – is 10 September 1928 =100.[11]

FT-30

The Financial Times Index, introduced on 1 July 1935, also uses thirty stocks and an unweighted geometric average. It computes indexes for (i) thirty industrials; (ii) goldmines; (iii) government securities; and (iv) fixed interest stocks.

It also makes available figures of dividend and earnings yields and PE ratios for the Ordinary Share Index of thirty industrials, numbers of

---

[11] From 6 May 1991 a number of the constituents in the composite index have been replaced, e.g. J. P. Morgan & Co. (banking and finance) appears for the first time; Walt Disney & Co. (leisure) replaces USX (steel).

bargains marked, shares traded and equity turnover. The index is calculated every hour from 10 a.m. to 4 p.m. on any trading day. Current year and all time highs/lows are also shown for the four categories.

FT-Actuaries Index

One shortcoming of the FT-30 Index, with only thirty constituents, was the impossibility of subdividing the market for industrials into textiles, transport, stores, engineers, and so on, to provide a series of comparative sector index numbers.

It was mainly with this in mind that the FT-Actuaries Index was introduced on 10 April 1962. This all share index had, at Friday 4 January 1991, 667 items with thirty-four industrial sectors. The constituent items are weighted according to market capitalizations and the daily averages are calculated arithmetically. The total number of constituents varies almost every few days. Earnings yields, dividend yields and PE ratios are calculated, together with previous year comparisons and *ex div* adjustments.

Thus a holder of, say, LASMO would have a four-way comparison to judge progress of his holding over a given period of time: Share v. oil sector index; Share v. share within oil group; Share v. all industrials index; Share v. all share index. The index also facilitates comparisons of price changes in government stock (gilts), fixed interest stocks and redemption yields.

FT-SE 100

This index has superseded the FT-30 Index as a general market bench mark in much the same way as centigrade (Celsius) has superseded fahrenheit in weather forecasts. It uses a weighted arithmetic average of 100 leading stocks in fifteen industrial groups (base 1000 at 30 December 1983) representing 70 per cent of UK market capitalization. This is the most up-to-date index of the UK stock market and includes a full representation of high technology, electronic and service sector shares. It is calculated minute by minute on a real time basis, instead of hourly like the FT-30 or daily as the FT-Actuaries Index.

That the constituents of an index are not weighted according to market capitalization (number of ordinary shares issued multiplied by current price) is not necessarily a disadvantage to the investor seeking a marker. For example, because BHV's market capitalization is 5 × WRH this would not necessarily suggest to a private investor that he buy shares in both companies in proportion to market capitalizations, though many fund managers now do this to ensure their fund's performance matches the index closely. The average private investor tends to invest equal amounts in various shares without reference to the market capitalization factor. Thus the FT-Actuaries Index and FT-SE Index may be overweighting the importance of the very large concerns represented, and are therefore not always the best yardsticks of performance for the private investor.

FT-SE Eurotrack 200

Yet another financial index number was rushed into service during 1990, the FT-SE Eurotrack (29 October 1990 = 1000), comprising 100 top European companies. This has now been merged with the FT-SE Eurotrack 200.

This new European financial index was launched by the ISE during February 1991. It combined the FT-SE 100 and the FT-SE Eurotrack 100 Indices mentioned above.

It is a weighted arithmetic average, with a base date value of 1000, using market capitalizations of constituents expressed in ECUs at the base date, linked back to 26 October 1990 (the base date for Eurotrack 100). It is calculated on a real time basis, minute by minute. UK companies make up 43 per cent, German 14 per cent, French 13 per cent, with other EC companies contributing 30 per cent. The basis of the national weighting was determined by the relative size, in terms of market capitalizations, of the respective stock markets of EC member countries.

It is intended that the new Eurotrack 200 will provide a yardstick for the fast expanding derivatives markets trading in various options, financial futures and warrants, and so on.

Finally, the USM (Datastream) Index provides a market average for the 413 companies which formed ISE's Unlisted Securities Market at 1 January 1991.

Economic forecasts: fact or fiction?

Any investor must by definition possess the capacity to look ahead and make forecasts of events, whether this capacity is developed by education and training or by instinct and experience – or, indeed, by a combination of any or all of these.

One cannot make even a brief comment on economic forecasting without some reference to computers. This technological Frankenstein was developed in a technical if not in a commercial sense in the United States during the 1940s, and possesses an intellectual potential of hideous proportions. Its value to the world in the fields of medicine, defence, communications, crime-fighting, commerce, construction, transportation, education, oil and mineral exploration and so on, cannot be doubted. But certain potentially dangerous aspects have to be taken into account, to balance its ultimate advantages – such as the creation of considerable unemployment and the difficulty of ensuring security of data stored within a system.[12]

The economic forecaster will obviously make full use of computer-assisted techniques to simulate a market, or the sales of a new product, or for the projection of existing trends. This statistical approach will on occasion be supplemented by a market or end-use analysis. Here is an example of this:

UK deliveries into consumption (petroleum products):

Estimated demand by industrial sector for:

Bricks	Central heating – domestic and commercial
Pottery	Motor
Glass	Aviation
Cement	Bunkering (shipping)
Other industrial	Electricity generation

If we add regional analysis of the above by standard region by petroleum price zone by marketing area, we are set up for a range of managerial comparisons. The logical method of forecasting is always based on volume rather than value. Price can then be introduced at whatever price level the company operates in its various markets, i.e. standard, cut price or premium. The ability to adjust price will depend largely on the effect of price changes on demand. That is to say, on the nature of the product or service, the strength of competition and the relative importance of the enterprise.

We then have the bottom-up industrial and company forecast, as opposed to the top-down approach. An example of the top-down forecast from electricity generation for public supply will amplify the meaning of this. For example, if we have three years' figures, the first difference (Δ^1) can suggest a provisional estimate for year four, as shown below.

Hydro Electricity generated for public supply in terawatt hours
(one terawatt = 10^9 [one billion] kilowatt hours) Δ^1

	1985	5.06	–
	1986	5.21	+ 15
	1987	5.37	+ 16
(giving estimated)	1988	5.54	+ 17

---

[12] *The Other America.* Michael Harrington, 1971.

This first difference method is not so ridiculous as it might seem from a quick glance, and provides a useful check on end-use analysis, other statistical projections and computer model simulations. This is particularly true in the case of large aggregates which tend to be relatively stable. Another mistake, which has been touched on elsewhere, is to write off a declining market by over-estimating the decline. The professional tip in the case of making forward estimates of big figures in stable markets, is to use absolute numbers *not* percentages.

One outstanding commercial forecast was completely fulfilled by subsequent events – John J. Raskob's now fairly familiar statement made in 1919, that within twenty years: the US would be the world's greatest economy; motors would be the world's greatest industry; General Motors would be the world's greatest company.

Can we perhaps provisionally suggest one for 2015? The number one nation must be Japan. The second and third categories are much more difficult, because dynamic technological factors are so interrelated with economic that it becomes impossible to isolate and evaluate different scenarios in any meaningful way over an extended period.[13] In the industrial spot we would nominate computing, telephone networks or pharmaceuticals, but in the company spot, almost anything could happen.

Thus we may reach the position that the economic forecast almost always differs from the outcome. To the uninitiated this generally means the 'guesstimate' is wrong. The forecaster in the field of business economics knows it can be damaging to put up too many forecasts, as people always remember the bad ones and often say that the correct ones were obvious to everyone. However, the forecaster whose continual observation enables him to get a higher percentage of shots on target than the occasional player is well aware that variances between actual and estimated values will always arise. Future systematic refinements of forecasting techniques will attempt to narrow those differences.

New products are virtually impossible to forecast with any degree of accuracy, as there is no statistical base data to project from, yet a forecast of some sort, using a parallel situation perhaps, has to be made for production, financial and marketing purposes. We may assume that the accuracy of any managerial or business forecast will be determined, *inter alia*, by the following factors:

1. Nature of the product or service
2. Price level chosen

---

[13] *Technological Forecasting in Perspective.* E. Jantsch, 1967.

3. Experience and skill of the forecaster
4. Application of proven forecasting techniques
5. The extent to which economic and technological relationships change over the period of the forecast. Investment collapsing in one market sector always springs up somewhere else. The question is, where, in what form and to what extent?

Basic factors influencing share prices

The three main factors affecting share prices are technical, fundamental and market sentiment.

The investor using a technical approach is interested in knowing whether there is a large supply of shares in a particular company overhanging the market, or whether market makers are short of stock. If NWA, a widely traded share, stands at 375p, that does not mean that the whole share capital of the company would be available at that price; 375p is the price of a marginal quantity of shares. If 50,000 shares were purchased the price might move up. In the case of a share with a narrow market, the price would be much more responsive to a 50,000 purchase.

The market is made up of a wide variety of investors, including those professional dealers interested in short-term movements, bulls or people who buy shares they do not wish to take up hoping that prices will rise to allow them to sell at a profit, and bears – people who sell short, that is sell shares they do not own, when the market is a little too much above equilibrium, hoping prices will fall and they will be able to cover their sale by purchase at a lower price.

Short selling makes possible a continuous market. If in looking ahead the bear foresees disturbing events, he sells short forcing prices down, but when he covers his short sale the market corrects its downward slide. The bull, on the other hand, operates as a check on the bear. When prices move too much below equilibrium, the bull buys and resells at a higher price on a rising market, and his sales in turn check the rise. Margins of both speculators are very fine.

On the chart (Figure 9) showing the triple top formation, resistance levels (chart points where sellers tend to appear) and support levels (chart points where buyers step in) are marked at 207p and 147p. The band between the support and resistance levels is sometimes termed the trend channel. For FXB, the theoretical resistance level is shown at 207p and the support level at 147p. As there are three peaks, the forecast downward

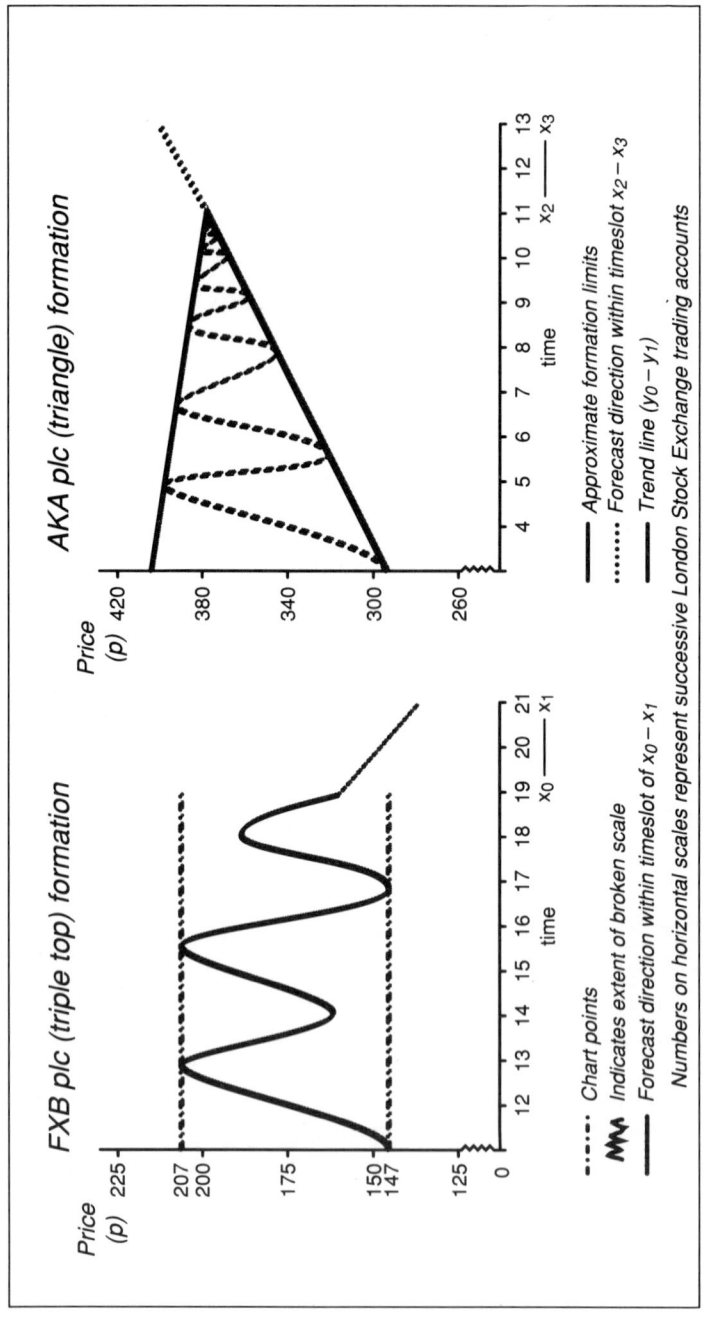

Figures 9 and 10 FXB plc (triple top) formation; AKA plc (triangle) formation

direction (x_0–x_1) is likely, from past experience, to be more severe than with the double top pattern.

The triangle formation chart (Figure 10) indicates a temporary exhaustion of supply or demand for a share, so that a relatively small number of transactions will have a disproportionate effect on the share price. As the triangle in this case is an ascending bottom, the forecast movement is up. The chart buy indicator is at time x_2, price y_1, where the range of day-to-day fluctuation has narrowed to correspond with the rising trend line, y_0–y_1. Forecast direction is up (x_2–x_3).

The work involved for a private investor in using chart analysis will greatly exceed that of an investor using a fundamental approach to share selection. But one should not reject the chartist approach simply on the grounds that it has a doubtful theoretical validity, since it was Roger Babson, designer of the elegant and comprehensive Babson Chart who correctly predicted the crash on Wall Street in October 1929. A fundamentalist, Professor Irving Fisher of IDEAL Index Number fame, completely failed to see the possibility.

The following chart (Figure 11) shows irregular fluctuations in the FT-SE 100 Index for two hypothetical time bands of one stock exchange ten trading day account in each case: x_0–x_1, a shake-out, x_2–x_3, a rally. Non-quantifiable economic and political forces operate, causing irregular or random fluctuations in the index. Sometimes these irregular fluctuations have no assignable cause. In other cases it is possible to assign a cause, though not possible to quantify the fluctuations with any degree of precision.

Examples shown on the chart illustrate the nature and effect of irregular fluctuations during two separate stock exchange trading accounts, each of ten working days' duration. In the first account designated x_0–x_1 on Figure 9 time scale, a shake-out occurred, the combined influences of entirely hypothetical events having an ultimately negative effect on the FT-SE 100, down from 1857 to close at 1738 in example 1; a fall of 119 points from the start of business on Monday (week one) to the close of trading on Friday (week two), i.e. ten working days.

During the second account, a rally, designated x_2–x_3 on the time scale, was in progress signifying that the balance of events was judged favourably by the market as tabulated in example 2, the FT-SE 100 Index ultimately showing a gain, subsequent to, but over a corresponding period of the shake-out. The Index registered an increase from 1765 to 1867 (x_2–x_3) i.e. +102 points, over the ten-working-day time slot of a 1989 London Stock Exchange Account.

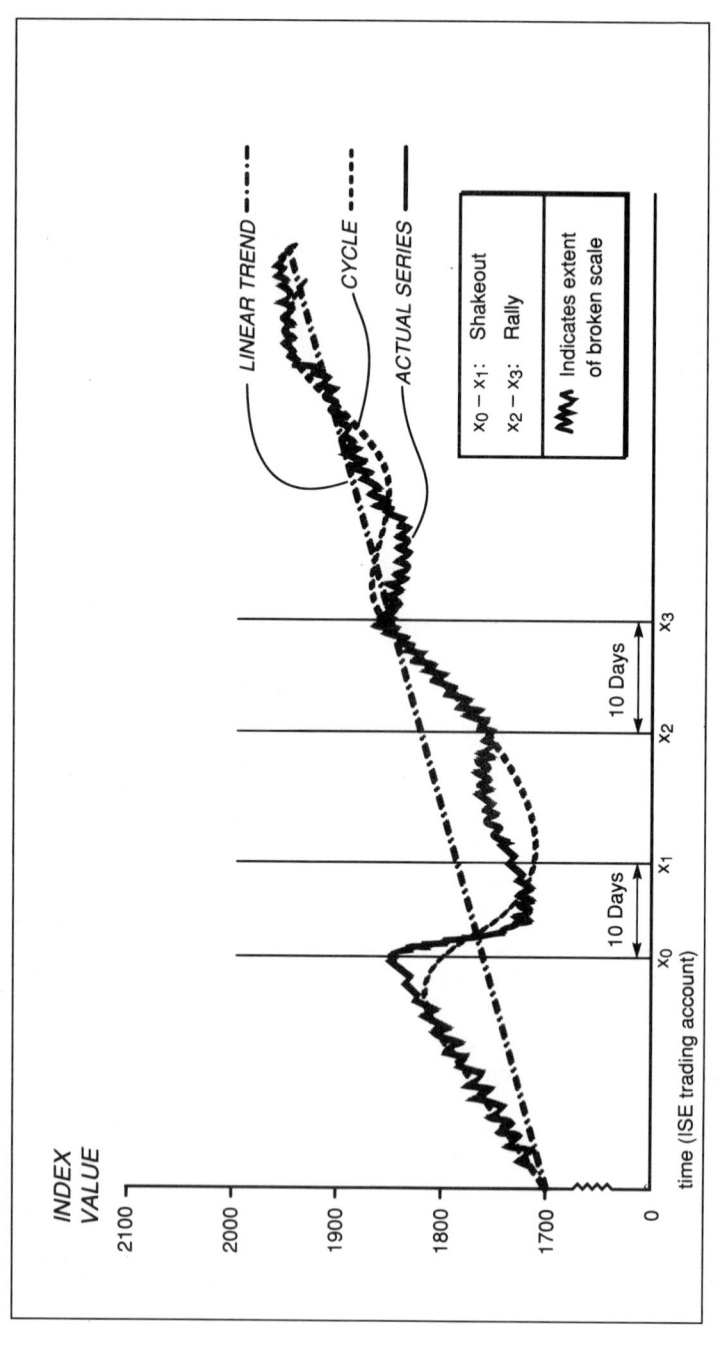

Figure 11, Chart showing FT-SE 100 index plotted against a linear trend and an approximation of a short duration cycle

Examples of fictional news items and their effect on the market are separately tabulated below for both the market shake-out and subsequent rally illustrated in examples 1 and 2.

Example 1 – The shake-out
Weeks 1 and 2. Figure 11: x_0–x_1
(Ten trading days)

News item	Estimated effect on FT-SE 100 Index (+/−) (n/c = no change)	Index at Start of Account
		1857
1. Good foreign trade figures	(+)	
2. Local government election worry	n/c	
3. Ryan's Behind the Rising Sun, market report warns of far-eastern trade threat in motors and electronics	(−)	
4. Inflation worry	(−)	
5. National Economic Bureau's Investment Intelligence Survey; 'unpromising outlook'	n/c	
6. Opinion poll shows Labour with 19 points lead; with a sampling error of +/− 15%	n/c	
7. Results from Anaconda PLC disappoint (eps up 67%; A. PLC outperforms FT-SE 100 Index by 59%)	(−)	
FT-SE 100 Index at close of Account:		1738
Change (+/−):		−119

Example 2 – The rally
Weeks 5 and 6. Figure 11: x_2–x_3
(Ten trading days)

News item	Estimated effect on FT-SE 100 Index (+/−) (n/c = no change)	Index at Start of Account
		1765
1. Sterling stronger	(−)	

2.	Mildred Pierce Kent Cookies PLC into receivership	n/c
3.	VAT harmonization believed damaging to housing, publishing and household sectors	(–)
4.	Arbitrage suspension grip case. Appeal Court ruling – perfectly legal	(+)
5.	Macready/Douglas Pathfinder Index of Buying Power, discloses increased profit potential for large UK retail groups employing new computerized IBM 'Golden Scoop' method of pricing	(+)
	FT-SE 100 Index at close of Account	1867
	Change (+/–)	+102

Chartists and other technical investors also make use of such standard statistical techniques as moving averages of varying lengths to correspond to short-term cycles in the shares, and these have been discussed briefly earlier. One hundred-day, fifty-day, thirty-day moving averages are illustrations, the application of which has been facilitated by the widespread use of desk computers. Other statistical techniques include growth curves such as the modified exponential, the gompertz and the logistic in addition to the analysis of time series, correlation, harmonic functions and reference cycle analysis.

Using any or all of these would probably be a time-waster for the average private investor. We may assume that their application will normally be confined to use by commercial organizations and public bodies, where it can very easily be demonstrated that they could be of considerable value in corporate and official forward estimating.

It is impossible to quantify market sentiment as a factor contributing to a share price, although its significance is undoubted. The market conventionally takes a twelve to eighteen month forward view and discounts expected future earnings and dividends. The valuation of a share in normal circumstances depends on the estimated present value of a stream of expected earnings rather than a company's estimated net worth at a given date.

Certain sectors of the economy and companies within those sectors will be in favour at any one time. Others will be out of favour either on a long-term basis or as occasioned by a temporary fall from grace when a share or a sector is considered to have gone ex-growth.

An examination of the FT-Actuaries Index indicates sectors with a high and low rating. There are any number of factors which might be damaging to the market rating of a share. An important element is political risk. Then there are fiscal changes affecting most shares to a greater or lesser extent – changes in interest rates, capital allowances, direct and indirect taxation in the shape of corporation tax and VAT and other customs and excise duties. Exchange rate movements will also influence certain share prices and cheaper sterling will help exporters; dearer sterling reduces import costs and domestic inflation. Uncertainty surrounding a particular company will cast a shadow over the share price. Substantial legal claims have adversely affected shares in asbestos and pharmaceuticals. Tobacco shares have been depressed by powerful health risk propaganda. And any area where investment has resulted in previous disappointment will obviously be viewed with scepticism by investors.

When the supply of and demand for a share is in balance, the market is said to be in equilibrium. When the market moves away from equilibrium in the short term, it is said to be either technically weak (that is calling for a downward adjustment to price as dealers are overbought), or technically strong, with dealers in an over-sold situation and the market anticipating an upward adjustment to price.

It has been said that a price is a fact, value a statement of what price ought to be. The true value of any given share is virtually impossible to determine. The method normally used for listed companies is to apply a factor to current year's earnings. However, the earnings multiple (PE ratio) will depend upon the nature of the industry; growth of earnings per share; dividend policy; growth of retained earnings; and the debt/equity ratio or gearing.

The value of a share may be expressed as the present value of a stream of earnings to infinity. Thus if a company's share price is 100p and earnings per share 12, the PE = 100/12 = 8.3. The share price has in effect capitalized the earnings on a 12 per cent basis.

When the current price of a share is a close approximation to fundamental factors, the share price is said to be in fundamental equilibrium. Economic factors are constantly changing and being reappraised. When the value of a share is perceived to be above its price, the market will be described as fundamentally strong, and brokers will be advising clients to move into the shares. When the reverse occurs, that is when the current price is seen as above its value, the market is fundamentally weak, which will encourage sell recommendations by stockbrokers.

In the theoretical market model every participant is assumed to be either a short-term speculator, a bull or a bear, or an investor, i.e. a longer-term holder. Fundamentals reflect dynamic or economic change which is difficult to predict in all its effects. Brokers' analysts undertake a continuing reappraisal of all shares they deal in.

Short-term speculators make their profits from a correct assessment of day-to-day market fluctuations, longer-term investors from an accurate forecast of earnings per share and dividends. Another characteristic of the market is that a large transaction is usually taken to be evidence of informed buying. It is also often the case that the market will be both fundamentally strong and technically weak or fundamentally weak and technically strong at one and the same time.[14]

Favourable influences on a share price include good quality or steadily progressive earnings, showing growth in both earnings per share and dividends; a well-covered dividend and a low risk sector.

The market usually exaggerates both good and bad news. Fear of the occurrence of an unfavourable event is often over discounted in share prices; so much so that when the event occurs the shares are frequently marked up.

There are also numerous examples of new issues which were considerably overrated and others of a fall in profits or cut in dividend resulting in an excessive marking down of the company's shares. Sometimes market reports are so gloomy that the word recession is heard everywhere. It may be useful to remind ourselves of the technical definition of a recession as a state existing after two successive quarters showing reductions in real GNP.

---

[14] See charts in Chapter 7.

6. The Special Situation

Recovery propositions

These are shares, once highly rated, whose price has collapsed because of a sharp profits fall and the expectation of further bad news. Recent examples include F. J. Lilley (contractors), Lowndes Queensway, Coloroll, GPG (Guinness Peat Group), Storehouse. Any payment of dividends is often questionable and will depend on two factors: gearing and the speed of recovery. Highly geared companies such as Coloroll and Lowndes Queensway found it impossible to pay interest on their total debt, which resulted in a financial reconstruction. Storehouse, with its very low gearing, continued to pay dividends, albeit reduced, as it steered for calmer waters.

Obviously an investor late into such shares at a high price will either cut his losses or stay in for the promised recovery, depending on the extent of the losses and his personal view of prospects.

In the case of Lowndes Queensway, the 95 per cent fall over eighteen months leaves a long-term investor with no choice but to stay in. Large investors and banks interested in a recovery stock will have to remain, often rationalizing their position to steady the nerves of private investors.

Speculators will often hold off buying until all the bad news has come out. In many cases the market pricing mechanism will have over-reacted to events, often marking the share down well below its true value on fundamentals. It is at this stage that large speculative short-term purchases become a feature, which increases daily price movements.

There are numerous examples of recovery situations that have been very profitable to investors – STC, Tate & Lyle, Johnson Matthey and Cape Industries, to name a few. Equally, there are a number whose full recovery has yet to result from treatment, including Arlen Electrical, Cullens, McCarthy & Stone and Stainless Metalcraft. Such shares should be bought by none but the brave, the knowledgeable and the fairly well heeled.

Investors should, however, spare a thought for underrated shares. In the over-analysed London market there are always stocks that trade below fundamentals. This may be because they are labelled low growth or because their earnings are termed low quality, since any one year's results is not regarded as a useful indicator of subsequent expectations.

Again, there is often a conflict of view on the recovery prospects for a particular share. Certain shares always get a bad press, whatever their performance. Sometimes this is due to accounting convention, which analysts and financial journalists find technically significant. In many cases the journalists have got it right, but long-standing shareholders with a good deal invested find it hard to accept that the value they thought was secure just is not there. Examples of accounting moves include consolidating results of associate companies where the shareholding is between 15 and 30 per cent, treating non-recurring profits above the line and thus increasing the potential for dividend distributions. Certain losses may be treated as exceptional by setting them against reserves instead of taking the loss against current year earnings.

Other accounting adjustments which are frequently the subject of comment embrace the treatment of goodwill in accounts following a merger, the valuation of brand names, lack of divisional financial information and the accounting treatment of off-balance-sheet debt of subsidiaries and associates in the case of property developers and joint ventures in property. Financial journalists are certainly human and if brushed aside by a company chairman when raising an awkward question or if not treated with due courtesy, a note of disharmony may easily creep into their reports, which can have a temporary adverse effect on the share price. The investor must of course be absolutely results-orientated and not rely wholly on the opinions of financial experts in the press who, not infrequently, shift their positions to keep up with events.

Takeover bids

Following the end of the war in 1945, the FT-30 Index of industrial ordinaries moved ahead steadily. There was no sharp fall in 1948 to correspond with the 30 per cent fall during 1921 – the equivalent postwar year.

The setback occurred in 1952 when the index registered a fall of 20 per cent on the previous year. From 1952 to 1961 the market had a good run with the exception of 1956, which culminated in the Suez crisis. From 1952 to 1956 gross dividend yields in shares averaged 6.5 per cent against average earnings yields of 18 per cent. Taking standard rate of tax at nine shillings – 45 per cent (1954–5) – the net dividend yield became 3.6 per cent: five times covered using the net to net basis. Further, a number of quoted companies were trading at a discount to net assets, and thus the stage was set for the emergence of the takeover bidder.

He appeared in the person of Mr (later Sir) Charles Clore, who first came to the notice of the investing public in 1948, when he acquired an interest in New Century Finance. Clore realized that share prices had been held down by low dividend payouts during the period 1946–52, and he had also noticed the possibilities of a number of asset situations. While his bids for Watneys, Gorringes and Grosvenor House all failed, he succeeded with bids for Scottish Motor Traction, Bentley Engineering (textile machinery), Furness Shipbuilding and J. Sears (Trueform). Clore quickly became synonymous in the public mind with the archetypal millionaire in the old-fashioned sense.[1]

In the 1960s other operators entered the field, including Jim Slater (Slater Walker Securities), notorious for the asset strip technique. SWS shares touched 412p in May 1972, attracting a wide range of investor support, but by the time of the proposed merger with Hill Samuel in June 1973 the shares were back at 240p. After the announcement they fell to 185p. The merger did not happen as City insiders were by then avoiding the stock. SWS had become basically a share-dealing operation (though they styled themselves International Investment Bankers), with operations in unit and investment trusts and insurance, and overseas subsidiaries in South Africa, Canada, Australia and the Pacific. By October 1975 the formula no longer worked, the magic had disappeared and with it most of the value in the shares. These fell to 8p, leaving a trail of puzzled small investors, many of whom accepted conversion rights in the rump of SWS reborn as Britannia Arrow (now INVESCO MIM).[2]

Other takeover specialists of that era included Sir Hugh Fraser, who made a successful bid for Harrods in 1959, beating off UDS and Debenhams. Lonrho obtained 29.9 per cent of House of Fraser in the early 1970s and finally sold its share to the Alfayed Brothers in December 1984. The validity of their controversial takeover of House of Fraser is even now

---

[1] *Bid for Power*. George Bull and Anthony Vice.
[2] *Slater Walker*. Charles Raw, 1978.

disputed by Lonrho. The MMC report was eventually published on 7 March 1990.

Among present day takeover exponents on the London market are Hanson, BTR and the most recent vehicle, Hoylake, driven by Sir James Goldsmith, which attempted an unbundling of BAT. Until it collapsed, this offered a first-rate example of leveraged bid technique.

Companies of all shapes and sizes in various industrial sectors are searched out by their analysts. Common factors include low PE, high asset value, strong cash flow, sound management, unfashionable sector, resource based. The bidder normally builds a 5–10 per cent stake as an insurance against failure.[3] It usually bids around 25–35 per cent above current market price but well below fundamental values. Shareholders in the target company are offered shares plus convertible loan stock or a lesser alternative of cash, and most UK resident private investors take the paper to avoid the gains tax.

Immediately the merger goes through the sale of assets surplus to requirements starts. Staff payroll is substantially reduced and the company takes a pension contribution holiday where the pension fund is in actuarial surplus. The budget office then prepares sales and expense budgets to a standard format, at the same time instituting an expense reduction programme. All operating divisions are then statistically evaluated month by month according to budgeted performance versus actuals, in sixty-nine different combinations of key management ratios.

Most shareholders in companies that are the subject of a bid are pleased to accept offers for their shares. However, accepting shareholders should realize that a takeover offer is invariably subject to a number of standard conditions, which include acceptance of 90 per cent of the ordinary shares from not less than 75 per cent of the number of holders or such lesser percentage in either case as the bidder may decide, provided that he has acquired shares carrying more than 50 per cent of the voting rights. Accepting shareholders should also understand that those terms give the bidder room to manoeuvre and that a conditional acceptance is never legally binding on the bidder. Similarly, the assenting shareholder may withdraw his acceptance before the bid goes unconditional. There have been one or two instances where a bidder has effectively gained control, but then withdrawn his offer because an unexpected fall in the market has made the terms seem over-generous.

The most recent example of a major takeover where this occurred was A B Foods' 400p-a-share offer for S & W Berisford. This offer was open

---

[3] Share stakes of 3 per cent and above must be disclosed within forty-eight hours.

when the October 1987 crash resulted in a 500-point fall in the FT-SE 100 Index in two days. A B Foods had obtained acceptances in respect of 59 per cent of the voting shares but decided, quite legitimately, to pull back from the bid. Berisford's shares – with the speculative element removed – fell over the next eight weeks from 426p to 287p. A B Foods controlled, at that time, 23.4 per cent of the shares bought at an average price of 292p, so its bid, if successful, would have effectively cost it a little under 375p (the weighted average price). After the later five for two recapitalization and change of style to Berisford International, the serious news about Berisford became public knowledge and the share price slumped in January 1991 to 22p.

We can now summarize the features of a typical takeover target and some of the methods employed for blocking the unwelcome bid. Shares of the target company sometimes trade at a discount to net asset values: the asset situation; sometimes the share price is below perceived fundamental values: the investment situation. A merger can also make sense where overhead reductions are possible in distribution and administration, and where production facilities can be rationalized. Agreed mergers do not yield much short-term profit for shareholders. The target company may have far greater value unbundled into its component divisions than it possesses as a whole. This is the reverse of the 'whole is greater than the sum of its parts', or synergy argument, and is basically an asset strip approach.

Hanson was able to make an attractive offer for Imperial Group in 1985 because, although Imperial was composed of tobacco, foods, brewing and wine and spirit retailing, the market gave it a low PE based on its principal tobacco subsidiaries (Wills and Players). This lowest common factor rating cleared the way for the knockout bidder. Imperial attempted to merge with United Biscuits, but the deal never looked right and Hanson emerged the all-time winner.

Consider for a moment a shareholder who does not wish to accept a bid, the non-assenting shareholder. These will form part of the minority interest in the merged company, and this is not normally good for them. However, under a recent change in company law, where the bidder has obtained 90 per cent acceptances, a minority interest shareholder may subsequently request the bidder to buy him out at the bid price. The bidder, of course, has always had the right of compulsory purchase of the remaining 10 per cent or less once he has secured 90 per cent of the ordinary shares.

An example of the form under section 429 of the Companies Act 1985, sent by the bidder to shareholders who have not yet accepted, is illustrated in Figure 12.

COMPANIES FORM NO. 429(4)
NOTICE TO NON-ASSENTING SHAREHOLDERS

Pursuant to section 429(4) of the Companies Act 1985 as inserted by Schedule 12 to the Financial Services Act 1986

To:

A takeover offer was made on 17th December 1988 by   Limited on behalf of   ("the offeror") for all the issued ordinary shares of 5p each ("ordinary shares") in   PLC ("the company") which it did not already own.

The offeror has, within four months of making the offer, acquired or contracted to acquire not less than nine-tenths in value of the shares to which the offer relates. The offeror gives notice that it now intends to exercise its rights under section 429 of the Companies Act 1985 to acquire ordinary shares held by you in the company.

The terms of the offer are 90p in cash for each ordinary share with an alternative whereby an election can be made to receive an equivalent nominal amount of unlisted   Loan Notes instead of all or part of such cash consideration. <u>The Loan Notes are unsecured and bear interest at a variable rate per annum equal to 1% below the London Inter-Bank Offered Rate quoted by   PLC for six months' deposits. The further terms of the offer are set out or referred to in the Final Offer Document dated 1st February 1989 which was sent to you previously.</u>

As these terms include a choice of consideration, you should within six weeks of the date of this notice inform the offeror in writing at The   Bank   plc, Registrar's Department,   which of the forms of consideration you wish to accept. If you fail so to do and do not make application to the court (see below) the offeror will acquire your shares on the following terms, namely, 90p in cash for each ordinary share subject to the further terms of the offer referred to above. The cash consideration will then be paid to the company and held on trust for you.

NOTE: **You are entitled under section 430C of the Companies Act 1985 to make application to the court within six weeks of the date of this notice for an order either that the offeror shall not be entitled and bound to acquire your shares or that different terms to those of the offer shall apply to the acquisition. If you are contemplating such an action you may wish to seek legal advice.**

Figure 12 Companies Form No. 429 (4): notice to non-assenting shareholders

Many shareholders, including warrant holders where there is normally a loss of time value, will know that not all takeovers are financially advantageous to them. Two fairly recent examples are worth mentioning. Ladbroke's offer in 1990 of 90p for Thomson T-line looked like taking second place to an expected bid of around 115p from Wembley. Speculators were in the shares at around 105p, including Hanson. In the event, Wembley could not arrange finance and Ladbroke's offer, to gain control of Vernon's Pools, was the only bid available. The shares slid back to 88p and the bookie, as usual, became odds on to score, ultimately securing Thomson T-line quite cheaply.

A Night to Remember, the story of the Titanic disaster of 1912, unforgettable as one of the best modern maritime disaster films and for the performances of Kenneth More as First Officer and Ralph Michael as the professional card player who could not help winning, had an expensive sequel in *Raise the Titanic*, courtesy of ACC. This epic effectively sunk the company, allowing Robert Holmes à Court's crossfire bid of 66p for the A shares in spring 1982, having first secured acceptances in respect of the directors' (mostly tiny) holdings. With the non-voting A shares then trading at 95p, having touched 158p during the previous twelve months, long-standing private investors, institutional shareholders and Johnny-come-lately speculators were all gasping. However, the bush telegraph must have alerted Holmes à Court that 66p was *not*, repeat *not* a popular win, which loosened his grip to the extent of an ultimate and grudging increase to 110p, with final settlement three weeks delayed.

Asher Edelman's conditional bid of 180p for Storehouse, subject to directors' approval, which was not given, did not look particularly attractive at the time (August 1989), especially when the shares had previously been at an all-time high of 425p. However, an increase in bank base rates to 15 per cent affected many retail sectors badly, with Storehouse falling back to 115p during February 1990. Looking back over those six months, the 180p conditional bid might have seemed remarkably generous in retrospect to many Storehouse shareholders, particularly with the *Daily Mail* constantly selling Storehouse short and piling on the agony. M & G Unit Trust, however, apparently do not accept the emphatic judgement of the *Daily Mail*, as they have been big buyers of Storehouse at around 140p, to increase their holding to 13.5 per cent. M & G usually get it right, and they see Storehouse continuing to pay dividends and eventually achieving a good recovery proposition. We shall see.

Another recent bid where professional speculators were caught off guard was by IEP (Sir Ron Brierley) for GPG (Guinness Peat Group). IEP bid 17p, having secured irrevocable acceptances from institutional holders of 60

fluctuated between 10p and 47p and stood at 23p at the time of the offer. Robert Maxwell, a 15 per cent shareholder nursing a heavy loss, was (not unnaturally) bitterly opposed to the bid, which seems likely to go through provided Brierley can get to the vital 75 per cent acceptance level.[4]

In the United Kingdom the investor and consumer, in theory at least, has the protection of the MMC (Monopolies and Mergers Commission) to which the Department of Trade and Industry (DTI) can refer any proposed bid deemed likely to create a monopolistic situation damaging to consumers. A national market share in single control not exceeding 25 per cent is used as an approximate guideline. What has been badly needed but is probably by now too late, is a supplementary regional monopoly policy – particularly for groceries, furnishings, hardware, motor spares, DIY, and chemists' goods – where large retailers have been allowed to expand unchecked, sometimes controlling 80–90 per cent of a particular trade within any recognized definition of a marketing area. The way has been cleared for them to get an unshakeable grip on many consumer market sectors. They knock out small local competition by offering attractive low opening prices; when the competition has been swept aside, prices slide up, forcing the consumer to take it or leave it. There have also been instances where customers have been offered free transport from surrounding villages to draw in the trade to these new retail areas.

Another dodge operated in some retail parks is obtaining a rating classification for these stores as warehouses, on the grounds that they do not have the display windows of ordinary shops, thus reducing the incidence of uniform business rate (UBR) and giving these hypermarkets yet more leverage over traditional high-street businesses.

The Census of Distribution, a detailed analysis of retail trade in Britain for the years 1950, 1957, 1961 and 1971, was quietly dropped. This was partly as a result of lobbying by major retail interests who, by 1981, didn't need a tabulation of sales by class of trade, by size and type of outlet, by form of organization, by region and district – they virtually had it all anyway.

We now come to the means available to a company wishing to guard against unwelcome bids. One of the best defences is a wide spread of long-standing and satisfied shareholders who feel part of the company. Since they provide the high-risk capital, this is exactly what economic theory says they are.

A current example of a company whose shareholders are very largely in agreement with company policy and the financial results must be Lonrho.

---

[4] In May 1991 Maxwell sold his 65m shares to Brierley, who then controlled 83 per cent, with GPG still suspended at 23p.

Alan Bond had almost 20 per cent of Lonrho shares in his 1988 takeover attempt, but he did not make a bid, presumably either because he could not finance it or because his holding was largely counterbalanced by Lonrho chief executive R.W. Rowland's holding of 16 per cent, with City institutions not a big factor in this stock.

Another useful device to prevent takeover is the cross-holding, where Company A is interlocked with Company B by an exchange of share capital, such that, at the date of exchange, the market value of B's shares held by A is equal to that of A's shares held by B.

A further anti-takeover technique is the issue of two classes of ordinary shares, equal in all respects for dividend and any residual share of assets in a winding-up, but having no right to vote at meetings. Under such an arrangement 15 per cent or even less of the issued ordinary share capital might have voting rights and thus control the company. This is the case with Savoy Hotels, where Trust House Forte (THF) have 70 per cent of ordinary shares but control only 42 per cent of votes, leaving the position deadlocked.

In the instance of water privatization stocks issued in December 1989, no shareholder was permitted to build a stake exceeding 15 per cent in any English water company before 1 January 1995. The Welsh Water offer incorporated the provision that no investor could do so even after 1 January 1995, without the company first passing a special resolution requiring the approval of at least 75 per cent of its shareholders.

Leveraged buy outs (LBOs) and management buy outs (MBOs)

During the 1980s LBOs of one sort or another became the fashion. They work like this: a syndicate composed of substantial investors and a management team, either based on existing management (management buy out) or an outside team (management buy in), is formed.

The bulk of the finance is debt and is provided by City institutional investors in three tiers:

1. Senior or secured debt (debentures) carrying interest at, say, London inter-bank official rate +1 per cent.
2. Mezzanine finance: unsecured loan stock carrying an interest of, say, Libor +3–4 per cent. Mezzanine finance can sometimes involve a parallel risk factor to US style junk bonds (high yielding unsecured loans), depending on the extent of the gearing.

3. A small equity base of ordinary shares – again provided by City investors for the most part, with executive directors making their own personal contribution.

It is obvious that such an operation needs to be funded on a rising market with a fair wind, to come through for investors. Any number have done so. Where the company enters difficult trading conditions caused by a collapse of consumer demand, owing to high interest rates or from severe unexpected competition, the high gearing factor works against it. Capital reconstruction became essential in the case of Lowndes Queensway, where investors saw their shares fall 95 per cent over the eighteen months ending in February 1990. Mullard Furniture Industries (MFI) separated themselves from ASDA by means of an MBO in 1987 and were planning a return to the stock market within eighteen months. But demand for domestic furniture fell heavily during 1989 and, in the words of MFI chairman, Derek Hunt, 'instead of trading down people didn't buy at all'. MFI was unable to service its debt, and a rearrangement of its financial structure became inevitable.

Others affected by falling retail demand during 1989–90 included Magnet, where the MBO was reckoned to have overpaid to the extent of £350m. Coloroll, once the darling of City investors, became a fallen angel with its shares plunging from 179p to 20p over the twelve months to January 1990.

Among MBOs trading successfully in early 1990 were Parker Pen, Kenwood, Caradon (builders' merchants), Hays, Rechem, Ferrari and Sheffield Forgemasters. Longer-term results in the 1989 MBO of Gateway Food Stores (£2.4bn) by Isosceles have yet to be fully evaluated; the indications are that it may succeed, but it will be a tough situation unless interest rates fall sharply during 1991.

Arbitrage and arbitrageurs

Traditionally the operations of international banks and brokerage houses, which bought bills of exchange or currency in one centre and sold them in another, were termed arbitrage. This speculation is made possible by different prices ruling for financial instruments in different commercial centres at any one time. Arbitrage between London, New York and Continental bankers in short and long bills of exchange was common up to 1914. Where the volume of exchange arbitrage was very large it had an influence on the rate (the arbitraged rate of exchange). This form of arbitrage virtually disappeared under exchange control conditions.

Here is an example of currency arbitrage between London, Paris and New York, with rates taken from *The Times* of 17 December 1907[5]:

Sight rates of exchange on London were, £1 = FF25.20 = $4.8615.
This implied a $/FF exchange rate on Paris of $1 = FF5.1840. For purposes of the example, we make the assumption that the $/FF rate on Paris was in fact 5.1863. The New York arbitrageur would have noted that if he sold dollars for francs, francs for sterling and converted sterling back into dollars, he would make a gross turn of approximately $55 on a purchase of $100,000 of French francs.

Accordingly, he sells by telegraphic transfer (New York/Paris) $100,000 for FF518,630 then sells the francs (Paris/London) at 25.20 = £20,581(London). Finally he remits the £20,581 to New York at $4.8615 to earn $100,055 − $100,000 = $55, before expenses.

Arbitrage margins are by their nature exceedingly fine, and such a transaction would not work in the same way today with electronic market links and instantaneous transfers of funds from centre to centre.

The risk arbitrageur had become a major factor on Wall Street by the beginning of the 1980s. He was, in fact, a big situations investor, who bought a block or series of blocks of shares in a company, where he either concluded or knew from sources close to the company that early developments likely to improve the share price were on the cards.

We should distinguish the arbitrageur, indifferent to the outcome of any deal where he is able to gain financial advantage, from the corporate raider, who seeks control of a company's destiny. Another leading edge market operator is the so-called greenmailer, who uses his shareholding to threaten a takeover, but offers the company under siege the opportunity to buy back its shares, giving it the assurance that he will never return. Greenmailers applied this financial submission hold to Goodyear Tire, who bought off the unwelcome callers. The company's greatly increased debt caused a significant loss of employment, a factor totally excluded from the greenmailer's calculations.

Other Wall Street arbitrageurs include Carl Icahn (Trans World Airlines); T. Boone Pickens, operating as Mesa Petroleum, who specialized in arbitraging under-priced oil stocks in the early 1980s, including SOCAL's (Standard Oil of California) takeover of Gulf Oil in 1984; and Ivan Boesky.

On the London market, arbitrage operations have been mounted in recent years in House of Fraser, Imperial Group, Jaguar, Berisford, Debenhams, Guinness and Thomson T-line.

---

[5] *Banking & Currency.* E. Sykes, 1918.

Of the arbitrageurs mentioned, Boesky is perhaps of greatest interest. He was financially interested in such major US stock market deals as the Getty Oil takeover by Pennzoil and its attempted subsequent capture by Texaco, which resulted in 1984 in that company filing for protection under Chapter 11 of the US Bankruptcy Laws, to avoid Pennzoil's claim of $9bn. Boesky was also interested in the General Electric takeover of Utah International, US Steel's bid for Marathon Oil, and Smith Kline's takeover of Beckman. At the time of writing, the largest successful leveraged bid of all time was KKR's (Kohlberg Kravis Roberts) takeover of RJR Nabisco, the US tobacco and food combine.

Boesky's book[6] provides a fascinating account of modern US arbitraging theory and takeover techniques from every possible angle, and will doubtless become a standard work for arbitrageurs of the future. He must have considerable intellectual capacity: he held associate professorships at both Columbia's and New York's postgraduate business schools. From reports, he was an entertaining and presumably well-informed lecturer; he was also astute enough to engage the services of a good informant, H. Levene, who must have come through time and again with the vital information at the appropriate moment. Whatever shortcomings Boesky may have had, he was a generous supporter of charitable causes until financial misfortune overtook him in the shape of the Guinness scandal, which became the starting point of a series of damaging insider dealing disclosures. With a peak annual income of around $100m, Boesky certainly lived up to the closing sentiments of his book's dedication: 'May those who read my book gain some understanding of the opportunity which exists uniquely in this great land . . .'

Here is an example of a share arbitrage transaction:

When the arbitrageur sees that Company A, standing at 300p, is likely to take over Company B, standing at 200p, he makes the following moves:

1. Short sale of Company A (the bidder), say 1m A at 300p
2. Purchase of Company B (the target company), say 1m B at 200p

If, as a result of the bid announcement, A slides back to 280p and B, the target, moves up to 260p, the arbitrageur has locked in the spread:

			£m
A.	Short sale: 1m at 300p	=	3.0
	Sale covered 1m at 280p	=	(2.8)
	Short sale +/−		+0.2

---

[6] *Merger Mania*. Ivan Boesky, 1986.

B.	Purchase: 1m at 200p	=	(2.0)
	Sale 1m at 260p	=	2.6
	Purchase and sale +/−		+0.6
	Total profit before expenses	=	+0.8

The arbitrageur loses only if the bid is withdrawn or if he holds too long and the bid fails. Even then B's price will probably not fall back quickly to 200p, leaving the arbitrageur a profit to offset any possible loss on the short sale.

The reader should note that the professional speculator will always withdraw from a risky situation when it starts to run against him. The inexperienced punter, thinking 'If others can win, why can't I'?, is soon drawn in up to his neck and becomes mesmerized by the extent of his potential losses, ending up a heavy loser. Arbitrage speculation is nearly always short-term, as financing costs are so high.

As we have seen, the takeover bid is not always successful, and corporate America has devised a number of ingenious devices to foil the raider. One example is the poison-pill defence, where a threatened company declares a dividend consisting of convertible preferred stock in the remaining entity. Increasing dividends is another good defence to which longstanding shareholders often act most favourably. There is also the so-called Pac-man defence, where a company counters a US-style tender offer by making its own offer for the raiding company. Another useful move has been for the company under threat to go into liquidation, which could be profitably employed where a bid still discounts net realizable asset value. Legal manoeuvres are also widely used in the US to block unwanted mergers. Such legal impediments are termed 'showstoppers'. For example, it looked as though the US legal card had been slipped in to the 1989 Hoylake consortium's unbundling bid for British American Tobacco, which was formally abandoned on 23 April 1990.

It may seem strange to the uninitiated that financial leveraged operations of the sort outlined are still legally permissible both in Britain and America, particularly when these huge speculators often remove gains from countries where the arbitraged profits are made to the calmer waters of offshore tax havens. For example, Alan Bond, the Australian entrepreneur and Americas Cup winner, with an income at one time running into millions a year, was reported as paying an average income tax rate of just 0.9 per cent (capital gains are always tax free or minimal in such international financial centres).

Some British takeovers must have resulted in big losses of UK corporation tax, a fact than can hardly have escaped the notice of the Inland

Revenue. A recent example was provided by the takeover of the profitable Dickinson Robinson Group (DRG) by a Bermuda-based company, which will undoubtedly represent a considerable loss of UK corporation tax in the future.

Some merits and demerits of shares in general

After a few years of owning shares any investor is bound to have his own list of pet likes and dislikes. For the benefit of those new to the subject, some unfavourable characteristics are summarized below, followed by what might be described as a hypothetical profile of a good share.

Unfavourable attributes include:

1. Infrequently traded; very small number of market makers.
2. Sometimes passes or reduces dividends or does not pay a dividend at all, offering stock in lieu of cash.
3. Consistently overestimates short-term prospects – share never comes through for the investor. Company springs a rights issue just before announcing poor results.
4. Share registration delays; late accounts.
5. The company is all jargon: profit centres, cost centres, resource, budgets and variances, etc. Skimming approach has a low rating among people who know it, but quite often stands high in financial circles.
6. Frequently shortens credit terms to its customers and increases the length of terms of payment to trade suppliers.
7. Usually has too much gearing. Management consultants always on board, destroying executive morale and charging enormous fees, often for very little, and sometimes for plagiarizing the work of existing staff.
8. Spends a lot of money on financial public relations, telling people how marvellous it is when the opposite is probably nearer the truth.

In short, a company essentially run by senior management for senior management; usually over-generous with executive share options and boardroom fine art.

Favourable attributes include:

1. Widely traded share; lowest dealing costs; many market makers.
2. Always pays good dividends, progressively increased in line with higher earnings.

3. Adopts a reasonable policy to employees. No excessive share option schemes for directors.
4. Has a business philosophy which attempts to harmonize the interests of shareholders, employees, customers and suppliers; consequently in good standing in trade circles. Reasonable approach to any customer difficulties.
5. Accounts available on time; efficient share registration.
6. Keeps shareholders fully up to date with events affecting the company, not simply inner circle investors and stockbrokers.
7. Company maximizes managerial and employee potential.
8. Has a definite financial personality, which generates shareholder enthusiasm. Does not worry every moment about the impact of this or that aspect of the business on City opinion. If the chairman or chief executive says so, it happens; shareholders know this and feel part of the team; after all they are the providers of risk capital.

7. High-risk, High-return Investing; Crashes and Crises

The common factor in all high-risk investment is that a bookie would lay against you. In other words, the odds are decidedly against a successful outcome for the investor, which may be compensated by the prospect of an exciting otentially high-return investment. An investor in this area therefore needs considerable experience in evaluating risk, coupled with substantial means so that losses – some are probably unavoidable – will not be overwhelming. They are not advisable investments for the uninitiated as in many cases the markets are technical and fast moving so that even limited exposure can be expensive.

Traded options

This is the right to buy or sell a financial instrument at an agreed price within a specified period. A traded option may be bought and sold any number of times during its nine months' life. The cost of buying an option is called a premium: composed of two elements, intrinsic value and time value.

'In the money' options have intrinsic value when the stock's current market value is above the striking or exercise price in the case of 'call options', and when the market value is below the exercise price in the case of 'put options'. An 'at the money' or 'at the market' option arises where the striking price and the market price of the security are the same, and there is thus zero intrinsic value. Such an option may still have value and hus command a premium whenever option investors feel that a change in the price of the underlying security will move in their favour, resulting in a higher value for the traded option at or before expiry.

The London Traded Options Market (LTOM – see Figure 4, p. 31) has expanded rapidly since its inception in 1978. The number of contracts has shown a surprising increase and the range of equities for which traded options are written now extends to seventy leading stocks. Also included are stock index options on the FT-SE 100, which, in January 1990 amounted to 25 per cent of turnover, options in two currencies and the new Euro Index option with a twelve-month life. Here the investor decides whether the index is going up or down, estimating the likely level during a given month and investing accordingly. In the case of the FT-SE 100 contract, the premium over the cash index during the last two months of 1990 varied between $1\frac{1}{2}$–$2\frac{1}{2}$ per cent or 30–50 points.

A buyer of stock index futures in the FT-SE 100 which subsequently gives him a profit will take up the shares to sell in the market, as the FT-SE 100 contract involves physical delivery. If, however, the deal does not yield a profit, there can be no delivery and cash settlement is by difference.

A key feature of traded options is that as a derivative of the stock market they allow investors to participate in share movements at a more modest cost than buying the underlying securities often as low as 5 per cent of total commitment. The essence of all options, whether on shares, currency or stock market indexes is that they limit risk, conferring the right but not the obligation to trade. In this way the profit potential is not restricted.

The following example shows that any given movement in the underlying security will result in a much greater relative movement in the highly geared option. In May 1989, 240p call options in British Telecom, moved up from 8p on 19 February to 43p on 2 April, against a share price movement of +52p to 292p: a share price gain of 22 per cent resulted in a call option rise of 35p (437 per cent). Here is the LTOM scale of commissions as at June 1990:[1]

Contract value

	£	%
First	5,000	$2\frac{1}{2}$
Next	10,000	$1\frac{1}{2}$
Next	100,000+	1

Minimum commission of £10
No stamp duty, PTM levy or VAT since 1 January 1990

---

[1] See p.31 for the merge of LTOM and LIFFE.

LOCH clearing charges — £1.50
Minimum contract — 1000 shares
Maximum — 5000 shares

Notes:

1. Commissions payable every time a contract is traded.
2. Very few contracts involve physical delivery of shares.
3. Quoted prices are the cost to buy. Spreads range up to a maximum of 20 per cent.
4. Contract note is evidence of the transaction; cash settlement: dealing Day 1, payment Day 2; most clients in account current with their stockbroker.
5. Time value plus intrinsic value = total premium.

Example of an 'in the money' call option

Underlying security	Exercise price	Series date	Premium
Jaguar			
Price 3 January 1990 – 848p	800p	June 1990	52p

Here the premium of 52p confers the right to buy Jaguar shares at 800p, so the intrinsic value = 848p − 800p = 48p

Time value is thus 52p − 48p = 4p
Breakeven price = 800p + 52p = 852p

	£
Cost of one contract = 52p × 1000 =	520.00
Commission at 2.5 per cent =	13.00
LOCH clearing charges =	1.50
Total cost =	534.50

Traditional options

These conventional options are limited to a life of three months, are non-assignable and are available only at the current price of the underlying security, i.e. at the market options. The key advantages of options are that they allow an investor to take some insurance against the effects of market fluctuation. For example, if he thinks a share is likely to move up in the near future but does not wish to commit himself to a purchase at that moment, a call option may be the answer. In circumstances where a shareholder, showing a good paper profit on a share, wishes to lock in that profit and possibly avoid CGT, rather than actually selling, he will buy a put option giving him the right to sell the shares at the current price during the next three months (see glossary and Capital Gains Tax, Chapter Five). Another tack is to sell and reinvest the proceeds in a high-interest account, buying a call option against the possibility of the stock showing an early rise.

The option player must have good background knowledge of the short-term and seasonal movements of the underlying shares and he must make accurate calculations of dealing costs. An outline of some more complex option strategies is set out below for the benefit of the more adventurous and experienced, who may be drawn to these sophisticated, fast-moving and high-risk markets.

Example of an 'out of the money' put option

Underlying security	Exercise price	Series date	Premium
Cable and Wireless 570p	550p	April 1990	25p

In this case a premium of 25p confers the right to sell Cable and Wireless at 550p. With the current price below the exercise price there is no intrinsic value and the premium of 25p represents all-time value.

Breakeven price is 550p − 25p = 525p

		£
Cost of one contract = 25p × 1000	=	250.00
Commission at 2.5 per cent	=	6.25
LOCH clearing charges	=	1.50
Total cost	=	257.75

For investors who may feel inclined to write (sell), i.e. to receive a premium in return for assuming a risk, alternative option strategies include the **straddle**: the simultaneous sale of a put option and a call option in the same series at a given price. For example, suppose 'at the money' calls and puts in WBX at 150p are 13p, provided the share price moves within limits of 150p +/− 2 × 13p = 124p/176p, a gain must accrue to the seller. At 168p, say, the call option is exercised, the put option expires worthless, hence the seller's position = 1000 × (13p) − 1000 × (18−13) = 8000p. In order to be profitable, the price must stay within a given range.

The **combination, or spread** offers another splendid financial opportunity to those quick at mental arithmetic. In this case an 'out of the money' put is combined with an 'at the money' call. Selling FXB 180p calls at 19p and 160p puts at 7p, we have a total premium of (1000 × 19p) + (1000 × 7p) = £260. If the price of the underlying security has moved between 160p and 180p by expiry, both options expire worthless and the writer (seller) gains £260. Hence, breakeven will be: 180p + 26p = 206p or 160p − 26p = 134p. Other varieties comprise triple options such as the **strip**, a combination of two separate puts plus one call; the **strap**, a combination of two separate calls plus one put; the **strangle**, the simultaneous sale of an 'in the money' put and an 'in the money' call; and the **butterfly**, involving the purchase of three different series at three different and equidistant exercise prices.

There are in addition a range of permutations such as **vertical spreads**, **calendar spreads** and **diagonal spreads**, all attempting to tilt the balance of advantage towards potential gain, thus minimizing risk in theory, while keeping the commissions flowing.

It is no secret that options trade better in a rising equity market, and many people in them will allow discretion to their brokers, as speed of action and proximity to the market are both key factors.

The European Options Exchange offers an extensive range of options on gold, EQE indexes and in leading Dutch stocks. Also now available are three-, four- and five-year long-term option contracts on such major international stocks as Royal Dutch Shell, Philips, Unilever and AKZO.

Recent additions to the equity derivatives market are J. P. Morgan/Salomon warrants and stock index futures on the Tokyo Nikkei (225 share) average. There are also long-term currency options on the Tokyo SE Index (TOPIX).

Index betting

IG Index (financial bookmakers) offers the investor the opportunity of betting on nominated values of FT-SE 100 Index.[2] The investor opens an account based on 5 per cent of his stake value multiplied by the current index. For example, someone wishing to play at £10 a point with the FT-SE 100 at its 3 January 1990 close of 2463 would open his account with £2463 × 10 × 5/100 = £1231, say £1200. Supposing he elects to bet on a March index value exceeding the IG Index quote of 2503 (sell)/2513 (buy) and closes his position with the FT-SE 100 at 2562 [IG price 2557 (sell)/2567 (buy)], we have:

Index bought (4 January)	2513
Index sold (22 March)	2557
	44 × £10 = £440 profit

[2] Extended in 1991 to cover speculation in more than 80 markets including gold bullion and pork belly futures.

Any profit is regarded as betting winnings and outside the scope of capital gains tax. It is important to note that if the client does not sell during March, his position will be automatically closed at the end of trading on the last business day of the month. Index betting contracts are legally enforceable agreements under section 63 of the Financial Services Act, 1986.

Investors should realize that since Big Bang, daily fluctuations of the FT-SE 100 have been much more volatile and the index itself much less predictable, both in the short and longer term. Programme trading can also increase daily fluctuations. No computer model is ever likely to appear that will give even a reasonable forecast of such a financial index three, six or twelve months forward (though doubtless some will make such a claim), as the mix of variables influencing the outcome is so complex, many of them being non-quantifiable and thus only capable of being assigned arbitrary values in any forecasting equation.

Futures and options

The essential characteristic of all futures and options speculation is that the player obtains a result, one way or another, within a specified period. These exciting markets call for the instinctive response of the successful entrepreneur or professional gambler. If you buy a speculative share in an interesting situation and a profit does not materialize, the medium- or long-term investor can hold, instead of taking an immediate loss. In the case of an option (traded or traditional), the holder either exercises the option or it expires valueless. In other words it confers a right to buy or sell, but not the obligation to do so.

A future may be defined as an agreement to buy or sell a financial instrument or commodity at a fixed price on a given date. Futures are traded when a buyer and seller agree terms, sometimes by means of open outcry on London FOX or LIFFE or via the newly introduced automated electronic trading system (ATS).

Obviously, substantial profits can be earned and much money lost in futures. However, it can be stated with confidence that there have always been many more losers than winners, as there always are with horse racing and other forms of gambling. The major difference with futures is that certain types of forward sale contracts carry the possibility of loss in excess of the original commitment.[3] Theoretically, this can amount to a legal

---

[3] Since 1991 certain dealers in futures have introduced a limited liability clause to protect the speculator.

liability without limit. One wonders just how many wealthy private investors have given up the unequal struggle to make a profit in the futures market, against the twin difficulties of accurately predicting market fluctuations within a given time frame and shouldering the heavy cost of contract charges. It seems on reflection that there can be only one theme song for the futures speculator . . . *Je ne regrette rien* . . .' Here is an illustration of a typical futures sterling/US$ contract:

On 8 February 1990 an investor, believing that sterling will strengthen against the dollar, instructs his broker to buy one contract (£25,000) for April at £1 = $1.68.
On 27 February sterling has moved up £1 = $1.74 and he decides to sell one April sterling contract at £1 = $1.74.

Hence, buying £25,000 at $1.68
        selling   at $1.74
     means a profit of $0.06 × 25,000
As 1 cent rise in sterling = $250, 6 cents = $1500 profit

Normally the futures investor in currencies or financial instruments, such as gilts or stock index options in the FT-SE 100, will be in account current with his broker. About 5–10 per cent margin of any contract will be required in advance, making this form of investment highly leveraged. The essence of such future contracts is to lock in the price fluctuation of a particular currency or stock market index over any given contract period (as shown in the example above). This can be a valuable risk management device for professional speculators and companies engaged in international trade. In the US and Japan the futures market is equal to the cash (stock) market. In the UK it was only 3 per cent of the equity market at the close of 1990.

Another means of spreading risk exists where commodity speculators form a syndicate. For example, if twenty speculators in coffee invest £5000 each pooling to a total of £100,000 for a six-month period, a typical arrangement could be that the pool will be liquidated at the end of six months with profits shared and losses apportioned. Often these pooling arrangements are set up on the understanding that if the value falls to 50 per cent of the original capital, it will be automatically closed with a proportionate return to the investors.

In the US, stock index futures on Standard and Poors 500 Stock Index, comprising 400 industrials, forty utilities, forty financials and twenty transportation stocks, have been developing fast. With a US stock index contract trades are always for cash; there can be no physical delivery and there are no carrying charges. Each futures position is adjusted to reflect daily price movements, with corresponding debtor/creditor adjustments made to the client's margin account, which can start as low as 5 per cent of the contract value.

The Chicago Exchange is the largest trader of stock index options, along with soya beans, maize, wheat and the perennial favourite, pork bellies.

NYSE (New York Stock Exchange), Wall Street is also a large trader in precious metal futures – gold, platinum and silver, as well as sugar, heating oil and cotton.

BIFFEX (Baltic International Freight Futures Exchange) – formerly the shipping and ship chartering exchange in London EC3 – now offers futures in cocoa, coffee, sugar, potatoes, soya beans and grains; plus the very exciting Gerrard and National Intercommodities (GNI) Freight Futures for dry cargo at $10/pt.

LME (London Metal Exchange) trades in base metals futures such as copper, tin, zinc, lead and also in aluminium.

IPE (International Petroleum Exchange) offers crude oil and gas oil futures, spot and forward.

Warrants; margin trading; hedging; the short sale

Warrants have now largely been superseded by convertible loan stock on the London market, but are a negotiable long-term option to buy a given number of shares at a specified price, before expiry. They constitute a claim to shares, but confer no voting or dividend rights unless exercised. Among the small number of warrants outside the investment trust sector, where they still feature, are those of Hanson, BTR, United Biscuits and Eurotunnel.

Warrants have all the characteristics of the traded option, with the exception that, in the case of share options for senior executives, this class of warrant can be exercised only by the individual concerned. Hence the requirements for successful investing in warrants closely follow those of the option market, where up-to-date information on the underlying securities and close contact with a broker are vital.

Buying shares on margin, although still operative in the United States, has been largely abandoned in UK stock markets since the late 1940s, US margin requirements having fluctuated between 25 per cent and 90 per cent since the Securities and Exchange Act of 1934.[4] At the time of writing,

---

[4] *The Stock Market.* Eiteman, 1969.

for listed Wall Street stocks the margin is 50 per cent. If a client wishes to invest $10,000 in Lockheed Corporation, he must have $5000 immediately available, borrowing the balance from his broker. Very few US brokers will accept margin orders for unlisted securities or any stock not frequently traded, as such shares are inherently liable to sharper day-to-day fluctuations than leading stocks and much more speculative.

For a margin trader normally in account current with his stockbroker, the stockbroker will hold all shares bought on margin as security for any unpaid balance. The broker will account to the client for dividends received and charge interest on the current account debit balance (at 8.5 per cent in March 1991 against a prime rate of 9 per cent). Clearly, this form of stock-market trading, like options and warrants, allows an investor a gearing effect, enabling him to buy more stock than if he settled in full at the close of the account. Minimum percentage margins on stocks and shares are much more rigidly controlled by the American regulatory authorities than option and futures margins and, as mentioned, are presently 50 per cent.

Of historical interest is the now almost universal acceptance that excessive margin trading was one of the major factors in the 1929 Wall Street crash. This had resulted in a dangerously high level of brokers' loans (up from $1.5bn in the early 1920s to $5.72bn at the close of 1928), secured against millions of shares of small, capital-gains-oriented investors paying 10 per cent interest on their loans against 2 per cent yield on their shares. As the market fell, brokers made additional margin calls on their clients, unloading lines of stock on to a falling market whenever clients were unable to make immediate cash available for the additional margin.[5]

Thus it may be no bad thing that the practice has fallen into disuse in the UK. While its revival might be welcomed in some quarters, financial prudence suggests that the balance of advantage inclines against its reintroduction.

---

[5] New investors should realize that bank loans for the purchase of shares carry a high rate (April 1991) around 1.75 per cent monthly, 23.14 per cent annual effective rate, against a base rate of 12 per cent; that such loans are among the first to be called in when the bank seeks to increase liquidity; and that an arrangement fee of around 1 per cent of the value of the loan is also often payable. The bank will either hold certificates in respect of the shares purchased or equivalent security. In either case the borrower will have signed transfer forms in blank to allow quick action on the part of the bank without further reference, if necessary. Obviously the nature of the security to be purchased will determine the amount advanced against a purchase. An alpha stock might justify a loan of 75–80 per cent, a Liffe eurodollar option or a CAC-40 (Matif) Stock Index future rather less. As a matter of simple arithmetic and commercial common sense, borrowing at 23 per cent on a share yielding, say, 6 per cent means the investor must be looking at a situations investment, not a long-term holding.

Clearly, the mercurial nature of the futures markets with their high minimum contract values exclude all but corporate and the largest private investors.

The motor manufacturer, Jaguar, has in the past hedged currency risks in respect of its export sales to the North American market. If we take as an example the shipment of 100 XJ6 3.6l saloons, Southampton/New York at £20,000, with an exchange rate of $1.50 = £1 on 1 January 1990, the invoice accompanying the bill of lading might be expected to incorporate:

1. Date: 1 January 1990
2. Quantity supplied and price quotation:
   100 XJ6 3.6l saloons at $30,000, cif landed New York[6] = $3m
3. Terms: 90 days net

This transaction means that Jaguar PLC expected to receive $3m or £2m on 1 April 1990, anticipating an unchanged $/£ rate of exchange ruling at the date of remittance. If the dollar weakened to say $1.56 = £1, Jaguar would suffer an exchange loss. If it strengthened against sterling to say $1.45 = £1, Jaguar would enjoy an exchange gain. To eliminate the effect of these exchange rate fluctuations on sales revenue, we will assume that the company hedged as follows:

It makes a three-month forward sale contract for $3m at £1 = $1.50. If the rate moves to £1 = $1.60, the loss on the New York main dealer's remittance is exactly offset by the gain on the forward sale contract, i.e. at $1.60 = £1, $3m would have yielded on 1 April 1990 £1,875,000 (−£125,000). To fulfil its forward sale contract Jaguar buys $3m for £1,875,000 sterling and makes a gain of £125,000, thereby neutralizing the effect of exchange fluctuations. The position is reversed in the case of an upward move of the $ to say $1.40 = £1, where the gain on the New York importer's remittance is offset by a corresponding loss on the forward sale of US dollars, i.e. +/− £142,857.

Before considering the function of the professional short sale operator or bear, we must distinguish between the real and technical short sale. Any person selling shares who is unable for whatever reason to attach the share certificate to the stock transfer form is technically selling short. At later stages in a takeover bid, as we have seen, a seller with a certificate will receive a slightly better price than a short seller without. Under a recent amendment to takeover rules only a count of actual certificates can constitute effective voting control.

---

[6] Export quotation including cost of goods, marine insurance, freight charges, unloading on to dockside at port of destination, but not customs clearance.

The real short seller on the other hand is a market professional who, when he learns of or foresees unpromising events and notices that a stock has been pushed above fundamental or trend value to a point where the market may be considered temporarily overbought, sells forward a quantity of shares which he hopes to buy back to cover this forward position at a point where the market has become temporarily oversold. The US margin requirement for short sales is currently 50 per cent of value. As the charts (Figures 13 and 14) illustrate, at the points of temporary oversale (below fundamental values) X_2 and Y_2, the bear is covering his short sale and the bull is buying, intending an early resale at a profit. At the corresponding points above fundamental values, X_1 and Y_1, the bear will be selling, anticipating the next short-term decline, along with the bull who will be taking short-run profits. These fluctuations above and below fundamental values are designated technical, as they are created by short-term influences, which in their nature fall within a close price range.

At points on the charts where the short-term curves intersect the fundamental trend lines f_1, f_2 and f_3, f_4, the market is said to be in technical equilibrium, which in practice lasts only a very short time.

The professional bear speculator in the shares of FRB will note that at position Y_1 on the second chart (Figure 14) the market looks fundamentally and technically weak. He sells short 100,000 FRB on 17 April at 307.5p; news of this large trade causes a markdown of prices and he is able to cover his sale with a corresponding purchase of 100,000 FRB at 300.5p on 27 April within the same Stock Exchange ten-day account, halving the broker's commission. Thus, $100,000 \times (307.5p - 300.5p) = £7000$ profit before stamp and brokerage.

Business Expansion Scheme

The Business Expansion Scheme (BES) was introduced in 1983 as a means of expanding the so-called enterprise economy. On the one hand the government offered substantial tax advantages to the investor looking for the creation of asset value rather than earnings, which effectively provided the entrepreneur with a source of no-cost high-risk capital for a period of years.

Official encouragement of the builder-speculator, the franchise-entrepreneur and the one-man enterprise combines a sector-by-sector approach with a regional approach. BES schemes representing the sector approach included leisure businesses, retirement homes, assured tenancy property development, shipping and some hi-tech propositions, and so on.

NWD-(25p ordinary)

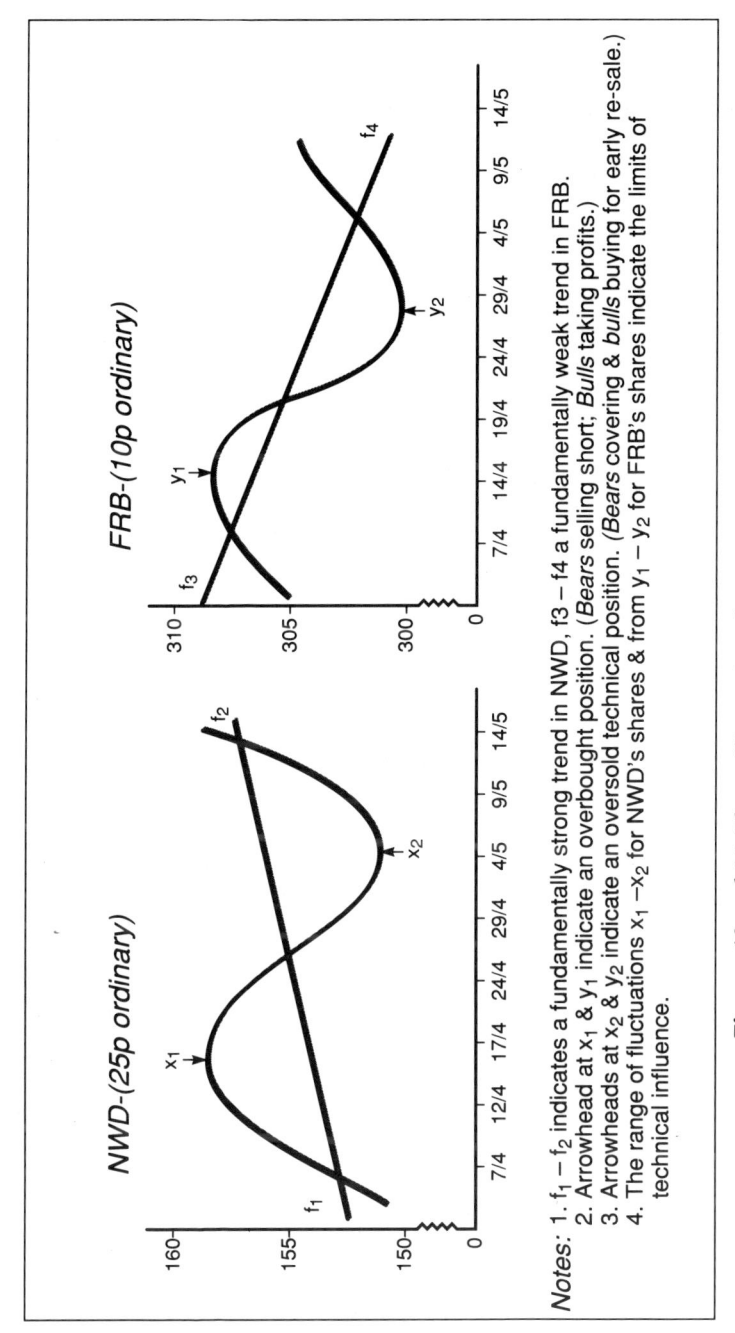

FRB-(10p ordinary)

Notes: 1. $f_1 - f_2$ indicates a fundamentally strong trend in NWD, $f_3 - f_4$ a fundamentally weak trend in FRB.
2. Arrowhead at x_1 & y_1 indicate an overbought position. (*Bears* selling short; *Bulls* taking profits.)
3. Arrowheads at x_2 & y_2 indicate an oversold technical position. (*Bears* covering & *bulls* buying for early re-sale.)
4. The range of fluctuations $x_1 - x_2$ for NWD's shares & from $y_1 - y_2$ for FRB's shares indicate the limits of technical influence.

Figures 13 and 14 Charts illustrating short-term (technical) price fluctuations against a fundamentally strong share (NWD) and a fundamentally weak stock (FRB)

Enterprise zones[7] or redevelopment areas represent the regional aspect of government business support. These zones, now numbering twenty-four, are located throughout Britain from north-west Kent to Invergordon, an oil port twenty-five miles north of Inverness. The economic advantages of siting in an enterprise zone include up to ten years' relief from business rates, no planning permission problems and 100 per cent write off on buildings in the first year, if financially advantageous.

We may summarize the BES qualifying conditions as follows:

1. Companies must be incorporated in the UK
2. They must not obtain a USM or main market listing for three years from the date of the share issue. By definition, since they offer their shares for public subscription they must be public limited companies.
3. Banking, insurance and leasing companies are some of the principal exclusions. Medical businesses, such as nursing and rest homes, are also generally outside the scheme
4.1. Investor tax relief is now allowable at the maximum marginal rate of 40 per cent up to £40,000 in each year. When the scheme was introduced in 1983, the maximum tax relief was 60 per cent. Investors are also offered the useful concession that investments before 6 October in any tax year can make use of a previous year's unused allowance to be set against that year's income tax liability, subject to a maximum of £5000. To qualify for full tax relief the investor must hold the shares for five years from date of issue.
4.2. No capital gains tax on first disposal of BES scheme shares issued after 18 March 1986.

The main sponsoring agents for BES company shares include Johnson Fry and Capital Ventures.

A number of points soon become apparent. In the first place, most of these schemes are interesting only because of the tax break, and thus will appeal to high-income, tax-orientated investors, who are fascinated by a gains-tax-free investment, having no immediate interest in income. In fact, the £40,000 BES investor needs an annual income exceeding £68,000 (top 1 per cent) to utilize the full annual allowance of £40,000 at a maximum tax rate of 40 per cent. BES is also a nice proposition for the entrepreneur. Instead of using bank finance at an average of, say, a base rate

---

[7] These were introduced in 1981. Some early designated zones expired in August 1991.

of 12 per cent + 4 per cent = 16 per cent,[8] less 25 per cent small company corporation tax, i.e. 12 per cent net, compounded over the five-year scheme period = 76 per cent interest, he obtains venture capital at nil cost for five years (very few of these ventures reckon to pay dividends in this period, if ever).[9]

Whether such an investment is of interest will depend on your personal investment criteria and the extent to which you can take advantage of the tax concessions.

Doubtful propositions and fraudulent investments

No account of high-risk investing could be considered adequate without some reference to doubtful and fraudulent investments. We must distinguish at the outset the inherently fraudulent offer and the offer where the odds are perhaps 100:1 against, but which is otherwise legitimate and may be attractive to a limited class of investor.

In Great Britain, where people do not lack the opportunity to obtain genuine, disinterested advice, it is amazing that so many put money in schemes completely and obviously phoney in concept, or which will clearly be a damaging investment. It may sometimes be the clever use of such reassuring terms as 'guaranteed income', 'fund', 'trust', 'an investment specially designed for', plus the persuasive charm of the executive representative which puts ordinary people off guard. Or is it perhaps the tea and chat for senior citizens at the comfortable hotel that sets the investor's mind at rest, contemplating financial security for life? The inexperienced private investor of mature years needs to tread most cautiously before investing any of his or her life savings in anything but a building society or big four bank deposit account.

---

[8] Banks have recently moved to a revised basis for calculating loan interest. In the example given above, 16 per cent nominal implies an effective annual interest rate (APR) of 16.99 per cent, debiting the customer quarterly. Under the new system, where the rate charged is no longer directly tied to base rate movements and is thus less flexible, the customer is debited monthly. Taking the 16 per cent example (April 1991), we now have an equivalent monthly interest charge of 1.45 per cent. 1.45 per cent a month gives a *nominal* annual rate of $1.45 \times 12 = 17.40$ per cent, but an *effective* annual rate (APR) of $(1.0145)^{12} - 100.00 = 18.87$ per cent. Thus, in the example given, banks have at a stroke widened their gross margins from 30 per cent to 36 per cent, increased the basic cost of money by 11 per cent and contributed a small but significant increase to the Retail Price Index (RPI).

[9] During February 1991 IMRO tightened the rules on BES schemes, restricting the use of the term 'guaranteed' and preventing forecast rates of return being expressed as percentages.

Among the many schemes – perfectly legitimate – now on offer to older house-owning investors seeking a higher income is the deferred interest houseplan. A typical scheme offers a deferred interest loan on 45 per cent of the value of an owner-occupied house or flat, with the assumption that by the time the property is sold, for whatever reason, the increase in capital value will have more than offset the rolled-up interest and mortgage repayment. The houseowner has thus preserved the initial value of his house while increasing his income during his lifetime. A major snag in many of these schemes is that once the accrued loan plus interest exceeds 70 per cent of the property's current value, it is put up for sale by the mortgagees, that is, they foreclose.

Now, 10 per cent interest payable on 45 per cent of a property value is equivalent to 4.5 per cent on 100 per cent of its value. Thus, if a current annual interest rate of 14 per cent on 45 per cent of property value is offset by an annual increase in capital value of 6.3 per cent (.14 × 45 = .063 × 100), there may be no problem for a few years.[10] But interest will always be payable, whereas increases in property values are much more problematical and fluctuate from year to year. In some parts of East Anglia, London and the south east, many over-priced houses fell during 1989 by up to 25 per cent. If house prices remain at a standstill for, say, three and a half years and deferred interest at 14 per cent on the 45 per cent mortgage is compounded over the same three and a half years, we reach the 70 per cent mark, which triggers the lender's foreclosure. This is usually a bad proposition for the borrower, with the uncertainty of a gearing factor always threatening to move disadvantageously.

The range of investments listed on the ISE – there are over 2900 main market and USM stocks – must necessarily include, as we have seen, many speculative stocks in oil exploration, all forms of mining, housebuilding, textiles, engineering and electrical, property, advertising and service industries, which might prove unwise or even dangerous investments for the average investor with limited knowledge. Many offer a perfectly genuine investment, sometimes of considerable interest to more adventurous, wealthier investors with wider knowledge and experience.

This is quite different from receiving a phone call from Geneva, Amsterdam or Gibraltar, outside UK limits of investor protection, offering specially reserved shares in this, that or the other fantastic opportunity. Almost everybody says immediately, 'Oh, I wouldn't fall for that.' Unfortunately too many have, particularly after being softened up with free

---

[10] Refer to Inwoods or other compound interest tables for an illustration of the effects of different rates of compounding over, say, five, ten or fifteen years on the hypothetical capital value of your home and on the mortgage.

issues of a monthly investment newsletter or other promotional ploys.

There is no way of stopping people spending their own money in any way they please. If a man or a woman goes into any investment understanding the full risk implications, that is a matter for their personal judgement. After all, many of the goods sold in everyday life would never find a market if people analysed and cross-examined each high-value purchase from every angle. Perhaps one way to avoid disastrous investments is to develop a set of financial antennae, which register RED FOR DANGER instinctively when a deal at first glance looks to be a bad investment for you.

Lessons from history

Panics and crashes

Speculation in high-risk, high-return investments is, as we have seen, not for the run-of-the mill investor, though it will always have a magnetic attraction for some. A look at a few of the panics and financial crashes in the past 250 years may illustrate some of the dangers – and perhaps convey some of the excitement.

The South Sea Bubble crash of 1720, the first-ever stock market crash, was caused by intense speculation in the shares of the South Sea Company, founded in 1711 to take over part of Britain's national debt in return for certain trading privileges in the South Seas.[11] George I was in fact governor of the company, which was largely the brainchild of Sir John Blount, said to live his life with a prayer book in one hand and a company prospectus in the other.

At the close of 1711, the £100 stock stood at 77; by January 1720 it had moved up to 128. By March the price had raced to 380. In the following month – in the great tradition of company promoters allowing as many people as possible to invest, further share issues were made and the price accordingly advanced only moderately during April, closing at 400. By May it had reached 500 and the public became interested only in the rise and fall of stocks. During June 890 was reached and the Prime Minister, Sir Robert Walpole, announced that he had sold out at 1000 per cent and advised others to do the same.

Isaac Newton, the great mathematician, recognized its fundamental flaws and refused to be drawn in during the early stages, but he eventually succumbed and was £20,000 the poorer as a result (about £900,000 at

---

[11] *The South Sea Bubble*. Viscount Erleigh, 1933.

today's price levels). Nevertheless, the price of South Sea stock kept rising through the hot summer of 1720, reaching 1050 early in July and 1550 at the month end, after the third subscription had been taken up. The tide turned in August, with the price falling back to 880 and crashing to 150 in September. The bubble had burst, leaving a trail of financial ruin in its wake: hundreds of impoverished share gamblers who had sold their homes and businesses to invest, and a few astute speculators including the Prime Minister, Sir Robert Walpole himself.[12]

There was similar speculation in the Mississippi Land Development Scheme on the Paris Bourse at the time the South Sea Bubble was building in London. John Law, a brilliant Scots mathematician, persuaded the French authorities to allow him to take over the National Debt on payment by the government of 3 per cent instead of 4 per cent interest, together with the right to develop French territory in the Mississippi basin. Speculation was enormous and the aftermath in 1719–20 was even more terrifying to French investors and non-investors alike than the South Sea Bubble collapse in England, as the notes of the Bank of France, using the backing of the Mississippi stock, became worthless, affecting millions of French families, not simply speculators.

Many nineteenth-century financial panics involved joint stock company promotions: that of 1825 was due primarily to a considerable expansion of credit connected with the new joint stock company boom of 1825 (joint stock companies had been banned since the Bubble Act of 1720, which was repealed in 1824). This, combined with excessive speculation in the shares of the Darien Company, formed to construct a canal across the Isthmus of Panama, and strong speculative buying of shares of companies newly promoted to undertake gold-mining ventures in the South American Andes, was mainly responsible for the severity of the crash, the worst financial disaster of the nineteenth century. These exotic stocks particularly caught the public imagination, banks over-extended credit to investors and eventually seventy banking houses were forced to suspend payment. In addition, about 200 merchant businesses collapsed. Young Benjamin Disraeli (aged twenty-one), lost a substantial sum which took him, even with financial assistance from his wife and Mrs Brydges Willyams, thirty years to repay. Sir Walter Scott was also ruined in the crash, with his estate disclosing debts of £34,000 in 1832. Earlier, Lord John Russell had offered to pay Scott's debts from public funds.[13]

---

[12] The Bank of England was actually involved with the South Sea Company at the time of the crash. The bank's agreement to take £3,775,000 of South Sea Company stock was subsequently repudiated in November 1720.
[13] The debts were quickly cleared by the sale of Scott's copyrights.

It may also be worth recalling at this point Disraeli's purchase of the Suez Canal shares for Britain in 1875. The Khedive of Egypt, Ismail Pasha, was in desperate financial difficulties and had given an option to a French syndicate to purchase his effective controlling interest of 177,000 shares or 42.5 per cent of the issued capital in the canal for £3.68m. This incorporated the onerous condition that the Khedive would pay the syndicate interest of 11 per cent for twenty years, continuing until the end of 1894, as he had already cashed the coupons on the stock for that period. The option was to be exercised by 19 November 1875. News of this arrangement reached London by 14 November of that year. Disraeli promptly approached his friend Baron Lionel Rothschild as the one man in England who could find the sum of £4m at short notice, which Disraeli thought the minimum likely to tempt the Khedive to break off negotiations with the syndicate. The Khedive accepted Disraeli's offer, and Rothschild made the sum available in three payments, the final one of £1m on 5 January 1876.

It was not a popular move with France, and one imagines the French syndicate had something to say, but as the great statesman had played no small part in keeping France out of a war with Germany earlier in 1875, friendly relations between the two countries were soon resumed. The final hurdle was, of course, parliamentary approval. As Parliament did not reassemble until February 1876 and might not vote funds to repay Rothschild's £4m, uncertainty was in the air. However, the Queen, the public and Parliament all looked favourably on the deal, though a few eyebrows were raised at Rothschild's reasonable commission of 2.5 per cent.[14]

Railway speculation

The 1840s saw wild speculation in railway shares. The Prince Consort, Prince Albert, is certain to have been among the really successful rail share speculators, having met George Hudson, the Railway King, for a briefing in 1846. The prince, notorious for his meanness, was a shrewd property investor, obtaining Osborne House on the Isle of Wight and the 17,000-acre Balmoral estate in the Scottish highlands in 1852 at extremely low prices for the time. He also bought the Sandringham estate, six miles east of King's Lynn in Norfolk, at a knockout price of £220,000 during the summer of 1861. Sandringham was intended as a home for the Prince of

---

[14] *Life of Disraeli*. Moneypenny and Buckle, Vol. V, 1920; *Benjamin Disraeli – Romance of a Great Career*. Sir Edward Clarke, 1926.

Wales (later Edward VII), and an additional £70,000 was spent on reconstruction, refurbishing and furnishing during the following two years, bringing the total expenditure to no more than £290,000. This was completed by the end of 1863, two years after the death of the Prince Consort on 14 December 1861 at the early age of forty-two.[15]

All three Brontë sisters – Charlotte, Emily and Ann, brilliant novelists and shrewd Yorkshire girls – were also railway investors. So was the author William Thackeray, a heavy loser as a wealthy young man, but a sporting one, as his series in *Punch* on the adventures of a railway speculator Jeames de la Pluche Esq., Lord Bareacre's footman, still testify. He also invested in American Rails on his visit to America in 1852.

The Duke of Wellington and his 'niece' were also holders of railway shares, causing the duke to seek most urgently on at least one occasion the advice of George Hudson on her holding following a market setback. Hudson, R. S. Lambert tells us, came through admirably for the great soldier-statesman with a perfectly legal market support operation that even later experts would have envied. The prices of the young woman's shares were increased as a result of Hudson's substantial purchases of her particular railway stocks. This was taken as a signal by speculators that something was in the wind. They piled in, raising prices still further, and on Hudson's absolutely legal inside tip to the duke, the young investor and presumably George Hudson himself sold out at a handsome profit.

Members of the aristocracy, government ministers, members of Parliament, judges, lawyers, tradesmen and many others rushed to get rich quick in the idiom of the day, via Hudson's exciting issues of high-yielding rail stocks.

George Hudson, a draper from York and the outstanding English financial personality of the nineteenth century, inherited the then enormous sum of £30,000 around 1827 and invested it all in railway shares, becoming the leading railway entrepreneur and one of the best known names in England. He gained control of a number of important lines, including the Midland, the York and North Midland, and the Eastern Counties. As he was to remind his York and North Midland investors, their shares rose from £50 in 1839 to the equivalent of £300, allowing for scrip issues, by 1845. Dividends of, on average, 9 per cent annually were paid from 1839 to 1848, so early investors fared extremely well.

Hudson paid dividends out of capital to the extent of £294,000, to maintain investor confidence in the struggling Eastern Counties Railway,

---

[15] *Albert and Victoria.* David Duff, 1972; *The Life of HRH The Prince Consort.* Sir Theodore Martin, 1880.

but he was forced to resign the chairmanship of the York and North Midland Railway at the famous meeting at the De Grey Rooms, York, on 20 February 1849 and, a little later, the chair of his bankers, the York Union Bank, which became part of Barclays in 1902.[16] His dethronement left him financially ruined, together with many York and North Midland investors, who suffered heavy losses. Intense speculation had earlier pushed up the prices of railway shares far beyond their true worth in terms of profits that could reasonably be expected from freight and passenger revenues, and the realization of this culminated in the stock market crash of 1847.

George Hudson was a character of his time and a man of ours, to whom cash was everything. Greedy, unscrupulous, he resorted to bribery, placed his nominees in key positions, manipulated accounts, beat Gladstone in a discussion on railway economics, swung Peel, that highly moral Prime Minister and first-class shot, on to his side; knew Wellington and met Prince Albert, as we have seen. When financial misfortune overtook him, he never disclosed a confidence, and bore his disappointments with dignity, as did his wife, no mean personality herself. Mrs Hudson's attempts to learn French were apparently amusing to London society in the 1840s, yet she knew those people for what they were, 'No better than they ought to be, most of them', and used impoverished society ladies as hostesses for her functions at Albert Gate.

Over the past 300 years there have been occasions when speculators appeared to have the whole world in their hands: in 1720 in France and England; 1825 in England; 1869 in the United States; 1929, 1974 and 1987 across the world. 1847, when railway share speculation was at its height, was just such a year in England. George Hudson made a contribution to our railway system which even Beeching couldn't kill off entirely. In any comparison with entrepreneurs, speculators and financial personalities past or present, Hudson comes out favourably. Against the gloating smile of Walpole ('Sold out at 1000 per cent'), the chilling ruthlessness of Rockefeller and Vanderbilt, the enormous power of Kreuger and the monstrous greed of dangerous arbitrageurs of the present day, he shines. For all his faults, Hudson – three times Lord Mayor of York and the Member for Sunderland from 1845 to 1859 – was well liked and admired, and a subscription was eventually raised in 1868 to provide him with a £600 annuity.

As Geographia's latest street plan shows, three streets in York again carry his name. George Hudson Street in the city centre was hurriedly changed to Railway Street in 1849 after Hudson's financial misfortunes earlier in that

---

[16] *History of Barclays Bank*. Matthews and Tuke, 1926.

year, to be renamed George Hudson Street in 1971, on the centenary of his death.

It is perhaps noteworthy that George Stephenson, developer of the steam locomotive, pioneer railway builder and early associate of Hudson, invested only in those lines he had himself constructed.[17]

Sir Robert Peel, an astute commercial man and, according to Queen Victoria, 'a cold hard man and a low hypocrite', who was Prime Minister from 1841–6, when railway construction and share speculation were at their height, appears to have ignored the investment potential of railway shares. This may be explained in part by the fact that Peel had inherited around £750,000 on the death of his father in 1830 (approximately £35m today), and obviously did not need to make more money. Peel, a man of high moral principle, might also have regarded stock market speculation as an unacceptable commercial activity for a statesman.[18]

Lord Melbourne, Peel's predecessor in office, apparently did not share this view; he is shown as a subscriber, residing in Downing Street, for £5000 in £100 shares in the proposed Midland Counties Railway. The Midland Railway Bill was passed in 1837 and the shares were soon at a substantial premium.

Crises

The financial crisis of 1857 was attributed to gold-mining discoveries in Australia and Canada, and the end of the Crimean War. In 1866 speculative company promotions following the passing of the Companies Consolidation Act of 1862, which allowed limited liability to any trading company including banks, caused a financial crash. This, together with the speculation in cotton following the end of the American Civil War, brought down Overend Gurney, the big London discount house, with liabilities of £5m. As early as 1853 the directors of Overend Gurney discovered a serious fraud perpetrated on the company by several employees. The effects were financially damaging to the firm, but secrecy and market confidence were maintained by not prosecuting the culprits. The firm's losses could possibly have remained confidential, but Overend Gurney had decided to take the protection of limited liability under the 1862 Companies Act and had to publish accounts, which eventually disclosed their insolvency.

The ultimate and probably least widely known financial crisis of the nineteenth century was the collapse of Barings in November 1890. In

---

[17] *George Stephenson.* Hunter Davies, 1977; *The Railway King.* R. S. Lambert, 1934.
[18] *The Bank of England.* John Giuseppi, 1966.

absolute terms the amount involved – £21m – was roughly four times the deficit which brought down Overend Gurney in the crash of 1866. However, to obtain a relative measure, we should allow for a 30 per cent fall in the general price level between the two dates. The true magnitude of the Baring collapse was six times that which caused Friday 11 May 1866 to be called Black Friday or Overend Friday.

When Baring's financial position was disclosed to the governor, the Bank of England took resolute and prompt action to establish a fund composed of the Central Bank, with joint stock and private banks acting as joint guarantors. This narrowly avoided a significant financial disaster.

Historians of English banking seemed to have passed over or commented only briefly on the significance of this crisis which, at the very least, must have concerned all London commercial banks and certainly involved the Bank of England. Acres, whose substantial two-volume work, *The Bank of England from Within*, takes its story to 1900, has no more than three pages about it; John Giuseppi's admirable popular history of the Central Bank from its founding in 1694 to 1960 has only one and a half pages on the Baring affair. Sir John Clapham's account in his official history of the Bank to 1914 extends to sixteen pages, leaving the reader at times with the impression that this is the authorized version. Individual histories of major English banks, published mostly from 1926 to 1936, barely touch on it. Fortunately for those who may still be interested a century later, we have H. M. Hyndman's *Commercial Crises of the Nineteenth Century*, which gives a valuable and lively account through the eyes of a City man who was there.

Hyndman explains that there had been an economic boom in the Argentine – and to a lesser extent in neighbouring Uruguay – from 1875 to 1890. This had created a modern infrastructure of roads, rail and tramways, docks and public utilities, such as water and electricity. Argentina's national debt had increased sevenfold in the fourteen years from 1875–89 to £70m. Further, many of the subsequently notorious 'Cedulas', bank guaranteed Argentine bonds secured on land (that most illiquid of financial assets) had been launched on the London market, at substantial profits to the sponsoring banks, including Barings. The magic of limited liability had also captured the imagination of Argentinian investors, as it had done in Britain some twenty-five years earlier, and this made its own contribution to the general speculation in Argentine stocks and bonds on London and other stock markets during the 1880s.

Barings were known to be substantial investors in various Argentine securities and were heavy sellers of gilts during the autumn of 1890. It seems the City's leading financier, the somewhat arbitrary Lord Revelstoke (E. C. Baring), chairman of Barings and a member of the Court of

Directors of the Bank of England, had been completely taken in by a North American adventurer who was not quite what he seemed. Lord Revelstoke was induced to believe that the economic potential of the Argentine was such that it constituted the 'Eldorado of the South' and that his company (Barings) should be in on the ground floor of this unique opportunity.

Baring's sales of gilts had not gone unnoticed by the market, and it was no surprise to City insiders when it was revealed that their acceptances on bills of exchange were running at an enormous figure. The £4m of Baring's paper held by the Bank of England, combined with the fact that the Bank's reserves were at that time no more than £10.8m, so worried the governor, William Lidderdale, that he contacted the Chancellor of the Exchequer with a view to considering suspension of the Bank Charter Act of 1844. The Chancellor (G. J. Goschen, later Viscount Goschen) was himself a former director of the Bank from 1858–65 (the only person, it seems, to have held both such offices) and a financial expert of the first rank. He decided to stand back and let the City of London bankers sort out their difficulties, which were not of the government's making.

The governor of the Bank organized an inspection of Baring's books, which confirmed both the firm's solvency and its inability to meet its current liabilities of £21m. The same or similar could no doubt have been said of a good many concerns which have had the misfortune to fall into the hands of the receiver and have ended in liquidation, principally because of short-notice withdrawal of banking support.

The next steps involved first, the formation of the guarantee fund referred to, headed by the Bank of England's undertaking of £1m and with substantial support from the principal joint stock and private banks, which took the total sum guaranteed to just over £17m in a few days. (In fact the guarantors were never called on to pay a penny.) Secondly, the Bank approached Rothschild's to use their influence with the Bank of France to obtain a loan of £3m. This was forthcoming; the French accepting Treasury Bills, introduced as recently as 1877, as security.

Finally, the Russian government was asked to sell £1.5m of gold on terms most favourable to them, which secured their agreement not to withdraw their credit balance at Barings of £2.4m. It is clear that these prompt arrangements avoided a crash which would have been much more serious than that of Overend Gurney in 1866, and prevented Monday 10 November 1890 being dubbed Black Monday or possibly Baring Monday.

Financial reconstruction of Barings was necessary and Baring & Company, the private bankers, became a limited liability company under the 1862 Companies Act, trading as Baring Brothers and Company Ltd. It was allowed a full four years to discharge its liabilities; all outstanding claims were settled by January 1895. (It may be of some interest that Barings, in floating Guinness's Brewery in 1886, provided the first instance of a bank acting in a company flotation, i.e. as a modern day merchant bank or issuing house.)

The editor of *The Economist*, commenting on the Baring affair, took the view that Barings had tried most energetically to deflect most of their liabilities on to the British investing public. This charge was never satisfactorily answered. Certainly, the Argentine Committee under the chairmanship of Lord Rothschild, did nothing for private investors in Argentine Bonds. It gave the Argentine government a three-year interest moratorium – to the considerable disadvantage of private investors and the not inconsiderable advantage of a number of large institutional investors, who obtained a release from guarantee obligations under a scheme to provide the City of Buenos Aires with mains water and drainage, which had collapsed.

Amid mutual congratulations by the government, bankers and the City of London, the governor of the Bank of England was granted the freedom of the City, made a Privy Councillor and received the official thanks of the authorities. Thus was the House of Baring accorded a second lease of life, enabling it to provide another longstanding member of the Court of Directors of the Bank of England: the second Lord Revelstoke (John Baring) who served from 1898–1929, and subsequently a governor who served from 1961–6 and was also British Ambassador in Washington from 1971–4 in the person of the late Earl of Cromer (G. R. S. Baring).

In the present century, the British government narrowly averted a panic following the outbreak of World War I on 4 August 1914. Bank rate was moved up sharply to the almost unprecedented level of 10 per cent; the August Bank Holiday extended to the following Friday morning; and a one-month moratorium declared on all bills of exchange and Treasury notes issued to maintain gold reserves.

There was no stopping the Wall Street crash of 1929. During the 1920s, as we have noted, there had been a real estate boom in Florida, which collapsed in 1926. Prices of US common stocks (ordinary shares) had, however, moved strongly forward over the five-year period 1924–9; in fact the Dow Jones Index in the late summer of 1929 was three times its 1924 average level.[19] Much of the share buying was on margin and therefore insubstantial. Irving Fisher, the leading American economist of the day, made one of the worst short-term economic forecasts of all time when he

---

[19] It is interesting to note that the 1924–9 increase in the Dow Jones average of 200 per cent was exactly paralleled by the FT-30 Index change from 1981, the start of the long bull market, to mid-1987.

pronounced, just two weeks before Black Thursday, 24 October 1929, that 'Share prices appear to have reached a permanent plateau'.[20] This proved a dangerously inaccurate assessment, and a wave of selling appeared as if from nowhere. As prices fell back, margin investors panicked and were wiped out when they could not come up with additional cash to cover falling stock prices. The nervousness spread to investors generally, and even orchestrated institutional buying could not check the downward slide. Thousands of small investors and brokerage houses were unable to meet their commitments and failed.

Speculation

Investors should clearly understand the nature of speculation, how it arises and then subsides. It usually starts in a particular market sector, quickly spreads to related sectors and then more generally.

John Stuart Mill, writing in 1848, gave one of the best descriptions of how speculation starts, gets a grip on investors and suddenly subsides.[21] First of all, there must be a speculative spirit abroad, a generally reckless and adventurous feeling. Secondly, it will be noticed that speculation acts on prices, which means an increased demand for a single commodity or perhaps for the majority of commodities. The third point, says Mill, is that at such periods a great extension of credit takes place. If credit did not exist and everything had to be paid for in gold or silver, the limits of speculation would be very narrow. Yet speculation, like inside information, is part of the fabric of stock trading, and neither can ever be entirely eliminated.

It is when speculation runs wild that it can become dangerous. The signs are rising prices fuelled by increased lending, with a slackening in the rate of increase as prices near their peak. At a certain stage, professional investors recognize the warning signals of unrealistically high PE ratios and quietly unload lines of stock. This shift checks the market rise and filters through to a wider circle of investors via media comment. Many private investors doubtless puzzled by the pause, and others probably anxious to avoid capital gains tax liability, will take no action and suffer inevitable paper and actual cash losses. Then as investors withdraw, the volume of transaction falls and speculation is checked. Further sharp falls in prices leave speculative transactions at a low level. Soon everyone seems to be losing as a result of the recoil of prices from the earlier peak. Investors seek liquidity at almost any cost. Confidence has now given way to panic, and distress selling is

---

[20] *The Day the Market Crashed.* Donald I. Rogers, 1971.
[21] *Principles of Political Economy.* J. S. Mill, 1848.

accelerated by sharply increased interest rates and the calling in of bank loans as banks begin to feel nervous.

This chain reaction of speculators forced to sell to satisfy their bankers drives prices lower. Third and fourth line stocks become virtually unsaleable as market makers move prices strongly against the seller, dragging the whole market down to the bottom of the cycle.

After a while, encouraged by lower interest rates and sensing a bargain or two, professional investors step in to buy. Share prices slowly start to rise; the business cycle is starting again.

Wall Street ban

Programme trading on an extended scale increases index fluctuations. It is now banned on Wall Street for the remainder of any session where the Dow Jones Index moves outside a range of ± 50 points of its opening value. Such limits are, of course, subject to adjustment at any time.

Declining stock markets

Private investors who have never experienced a falling market should not panic and sell everything at the first sign of a setback. The situation should be carefully and quickly examined to determine the nature of the fall. If it looks like a random short term shake-out, the best course is usually a standstill until the situation clarifies.

If the slide is widely considered to be a cyclical downturn of the four-phase business cycle comprising prosperity, recession, depression and recovery, the investor will need to consider his position more closely. Historical studies have shown that cyclical fluctuations vary both in their intensity – the maximum extent of market fluctuations – and in their duration, which makes recovery predictions difficult. Private investors may care to note that a cyclical downturn is often followed by a recoil of share prices of up to 60 per cent within eighteen to twenty-four months after the bottom of the cycle has been reached.

Perhaps the greatest difficulty facing private investors is when sharp falls in such market indicators as stock price indices, numbers of share transactions, traded option activity and so on, are seen as the start of an extended period of declining share values. This occurred on the London market between July 1973 and January 1975, when the FT-30 Index fell more than 70 per cent, to register 143 during that January. This index figure was much lower in *real terms* than the recorded *nominal* all-time low of 49.4, as Table 4 illustrates.

Table 4

DATE	FT-30 Index (actual)	FT-30 Index adjusted for inflation
1 July 1935	100	100
26 June 1940 (Dunkirk evacuation)	49.4 (Recorded all-time low)	38
January 1975	143	24*

*Real all-time low.

Since Big Bang, automatic selling of baskets of shares at pre-set price levels (programme trades) have made daily market fluctuations that much sharper. In a falling market, their effect is guaranteed to make private investors nervous, thus encouraging selling, which triggers further falls and the next tranche of programme trades, driving the market down to often unrealistically low levels. In effect, remembering the P = me equation, price (P) is being reduced because of sharp judgemental reductions by market makers in (m) the multiplier, as earnings (e) have not yet had time to signal bad news in the case of many stocks. The market's forward look anticipates lower earnings.

In such circumstances it can be right to sell and go back in lower down. Capital gains tax is the major complicating factor here for the UK private investor. There is no such problem for the IOM domiciled taxpayer or the K-list Jersey resident, who are not subject to CGT. However, for the UK resident investor this could be the moment to lock in some profit before it disappears altogether, making full use of gains tax exemption, combined with any agreed losses as offsets to minimize tax payments.

As we have noted, many professional investors and arbitrageurs will have left the stage some months earlier. For a number of long-term investors this may be seen as no time to sell major stocks or unit trusts as dividends should be maintained. Fund managers and other large institutional investors will also hold on; they cannot sell, because a declining market could not absorb large lines of stock without collapsing altogether.

Glossary

Account	Period of Stock Exchange trading, normally ten working days (see Chapter Two for new rolling four-day settlement)
Account trading	Buying and selling shares within the same stock exchange account. Settlement is by difference
Advance Corporation Tax (ACT)	Deducted from dividends and offsetable against mainstream tax liability of the company
American Depository Receipts (ADRs)	Receipts for foreign stocks owned by a bank's customers. ADRs are negotiable and a number of issues are quoted on Wall Street. The banks monitor the shares and collect dividends, which saves the physical transfer of certificates. Large British investors have been using the system to avoid higher London dealing costs and stamp duty. The 1986 Budget proposed a 5 per cent tax on ADRs originating in the UK; this was later cut to 1.5 per cent. Certain leading British shares are traded in this form on Wall Street. Dividend payments are made in dollars by the depository banks, less 15 per cent withholding tax to US residents
Arbitrageur	Buyer of a large block of shares in a special situation investment, where early developments are expected
Attributable net profit	Net profit after tax and minority interest
Average cost of capital	Weighted average cost of a particular company's capital structure of ordinary shares, preference shares, debentures and other loan stock

Balance sheet	Summary of a company's assets and source of capital (liabilities) at a particular date
Bear	Speculator who sells shares he does not possess expecting the price to fall to enable him subsequently to buy in the shares at a lower price
Bearer stock	Securities not recorded on the company's register. The property in them is transferred when handed from seller to buyer. Dividends are claimed by returning coupons (warrants) attached to the certificate
Bed and Breakfast	Sale and repurchase of shares on which a loss is shown. This established loss can be set off against a current capital gains tax (CGT) liability. Such transactions usually occur at the close of the tax year. Not all stockbrokers will undertake these deals
Below the line item	Non-recurring expenditure or gain, becoming a special adjustment to attributable net profit. Usually described as extraordinary or exceptional
Beta factor	Computer-assisted statistical calculation averaging share price fluctuations against trend values
Block trader	Dealer in large lines of stock on or off the market
Blue chip	Widely traded share of a large company listed on the stock market
Broker	Acts as an agent for investors in the buying and selling of shares
Bull	Speculator who buys shares he does not wish to take up, hoping prices will rise to enable him to resell at a profit in the short term
Cash flow	The net balance positive (credit) or negative (debit) of cash outflow (wages, materials, overheads, corporation tax, dividends, etc.) *deducted* from cash inflow (cash sales, cash received from debtors, revenue from asset sales, etc.), over a specified trading period
Chartism	Systematic method of predicting the direction of share price movements from charts and associated technical information
Chinese wall	A dubious convention which attempts to restrict information available to one department from other departments within the same firm
Churning	Excessive sales and purchases of stocks and bonds within a client's portfolio, where a stockbroker or other intermediary has full discretion and seeks to maximize his own commission rather than to protect the financial interests of his client.

Concert party	Associates of the takeover bidder who have pledged acceptance in respect of shares under their control. Bound by the same rules as the bidder
Convertible loan stock	Secured or unsecured loan stock giving a fixed interest return and a right of conversion into ordinary shares at a fixed rate, within certain future dates
Coupon rate	Nominal rate of interest payable on a fixed interest security
Cover	Net after tax profits + ACT recoverable divided by gross dividend, i.e. net dividend paid plus tax credit of 25 per cent in 1991–2
Database	A store of information in any field. Such records are now usually in computerized form, i.e. on disc, magnetic or paper tape, although this is not yet universal
Deal stock	A share whose price is influenced by arbitrage operations or takeover possibilities
Debenture	Loan stock issued by a company as a fixed or floating charge on its assets
Discounted Cash Flow (DCF)	Technique that discounts expected future earnings or expenditures to their present values at time zero (now). It is sometimes termed marginal efficiency of capital or the internal rate of return
Divestment	The elimination of unprofitable activities
Dividend yield	Gross dividend expressed as a percentage of a share's current market price
Dual capacity	Where a stockbroking firm combines both broking and market making functions
Equity	Ordinary share capital of a company. In a winding-up ordinary (equity) shareholders are normally entitled to the net residual value of any assets after all other liabilities have been discharged
Euro currency bonds	Fixed interest securities including convertible loan stocks, where the issue is in bearer form and interest paid gross
Ex all	Where there has been a recapitalization of mixed scrip and rights issues and shareholders have received their documents
Ex div (XD)	Shares marked XD are sold on the understanding that the seller retains the recently declared dividend payable after the date of transfer
Ex rights (XR)	Following a rights issue, when all shareholders have received their letters of rights allotment the shares are marked XR

Ex scrip (XC – ex capitalization)	Following a scrip issue, when all shareholders have received their bonus share certificates, shares are marked XC
Financial Ombudsman	The ombudsman, Scandinavian in concept, is an independent referee funded by the state to rule in certain circumstances on issues involving a private citizen and the state. In Britain this is the Parliamentary Commissioner for Administration, Queen Anne's Gate, London SW1H 9AB (Tel. 071-276-3000), who will rule on request, when he considers his intervention justified, on a wide range of matters where a private individual might otherwise be oppressed by the state or any large corporate body. An important area lying outside his authority, however, appears to concern disputes between private taxpayers and the Inland Revenue or HM Customs and Excise. In recent years a number of specialist financial ombudsmen have been established by the appropriate financial institutions to protect the interests of shareholders, insurance policy holders, bank and building society depositors, unit trust investors, and so on. Their addresses at 1 January 1991 were: Banking Ombudsman, Citadel House, 5–11 Fetter Lane, London EC4A 1BR Building Societies Ombudsman, Grosvenor Gardens House, 35–37 Grosvenor Gardens, London SW1W 0BS Unit Trust and Insurance Ombudsman, 31 Southampton Row, London WC1B 5HJ Financial Intermediaries,[1] IMRO Referee, 3 Royal Exchange Buildings, London EC3Y 3NL
Fixed charge	Debenture secured on specific tangible fixed assets, usually freehold land or buildings
Floating charge	Debenture floating over all the assets of a company, attaching to these in the event of default, and giving the holder the right to appoint a receiver
Franchise	The exclusive right to market a product or service within a defined geographical area for a specified period, in exchange for the advance payment of a lump sum plus, usually, a percentage of turnover, in addition to the obligation to buy product or service items from the vendor of the franchise. Bank finance can generally be obtained to assist the purchase of a sound and valuable franchise concession. The purchaser will need to demonstrate to the lender both his basic commercial ability and the availability of adequate starting capital

---

[1] Registered stockbrokers, insurance and mortgage brokers, investment advisers, company promoters, financial agents, etc.

Fundamentals	Estimated perceived value of a share taking account of growth of earnings, dividends and their quality or stability. Fundamentals influence share prices in the medium and longer term (see also technical position)
Gearing	Ratio of loan stock and other secured and unsecured debt to shareholders' funds
Gilt-edged	British government fixed interest securities
High value added operations	Any company or industry operating on wide gross margins, e.g. pharmaceuticals and speciality chemicals, banking, hotels, tourism, medical businesses, restaurants, antique furniture, fine art, stamps and coins, etc. Switzerland is the spiritual home of high value added
Index number	Statistical device for measuring changes in prices and other variables between different dates or periods
Insider trading	Legal restriction imposed by sections 68–73 of the 1980 Companies Act to prevent directors, executives and other connected persons from dealing in shares when they are deemed to be in possession of price sensitive information. Sections 25–32 of the 1967 Companies Act also prevent a director from dealing in options in his company's shares. These provisions *do not affect company share option* schemes specifically for directors and senior executives. Insider trading carries a maximum sentence of seven years' imprisonment
Investment trust	Many investment trusts are listed on the Stock Exchange. Their shares are a direct stock market investment and bought and sold in the same way as the shares of any other listed company. Investment trusts are quoted in the financial press; their stock-in-trade is the shares of other companies. The valuation of an investment trust share is largely based on two factors: (a) the value of its investments, and (b) its earnings per ordinary share or management record. Usually, the quoted share price will stand at a discount to its net assets per share. This discount averaged 18 per cent in December 1990
Junk bonds	High-yielding low-grade bonds whose actual security is poor, or conditional upon the acquisition of assets via takeover (see mezzanine finance). In the US, junk bonds account for approximately 25 per cent of the total rated bond market
Level playing field demand	Organized request for reinstatement of a former advantage
Leveraged buy out (LBO)	Any bid for a company, largely debt financed, with a small equity base partially contributed by management
Management buy out (MBO)	A purchase by the existing management; a buy in by a new management nominated by the takeover bidder

Market capitalization	Number of issued ordinary shares multiplied by their current price
Marketing	'The systematic creation of misperceptions'
Market maker	Wholesale share trader who makes a market in a range of stocks
Matched bargain (MB)	In a narrow market a sale can be effected only where an individual seller and buyer can be put into contact, either by a broker or via the secretary of the company whose shares are being traded. Many delta stocks fall into this category, which is a serious disadvantage where a seller seeks an early disposal of his holding
Mezzanine finance	Higher yielding unsecured loan stock
Minority interest	Arises where a group owns less than 100 per cent interest in any of its subsidiaries and represents the minority shareholders' proportion of capital and reserves. Private investors in a takeover often intentionally refuse to accept a bid knowing compulsory purchase is inevitable, because the timing of the bid is unfavourable to them for capital gains tax purposes
Negative yield	Where the real return on investment is below zero per cent per annum
Offer document	Takeover offer details sent to all ordinary and preference shareholders in the target company
Ombudsman	See financial ombudsman
Option	Right to buy or sell shares at a stated price within a specified period (see also shadow option)
PE ratio (multiple)	Current share price divided by net earnings per share after tax. This is the net basis of calculation, where ACT is fully recoverable
Placing	Sale of a large block of shares avoiding the market. Also a new issue made available to nominated investors only. Price may be above or more likely below the market price
Profit and loss account	An accounting statement for a period (usually twelve months) starting with gross profit and deducting all business expenses and depreciation. The balance is then net profit before tax for the review period

Programme trading	A computerized system of share trading by which estimated future values of stocks are charted against their perceived present values. When the chart indicates existing values significantly above future values an automatic sell signal is shown. When existing values appear significantly below expected future values a buy signal is indicated. An alternative meaning is the purchase or sale of a basket of shares at an agreed level of the FT-SE 100 Index or other financial indicator
Prospectus	A document issued by a public company inviting the public to subscribe to its shares. By definition, a private limited company cannot issue a prospectus as it cannot legally offer its shares to the public
Punter	An individual who likes to think he is financially aware, having grasped most of his legal rights, but not his obligations, e.g. under personal guarantees or unlimited liability. Expects all his shares to beat the index
Put through (PT)	Purchase and sale between two clients of the same broker. As the transaction does not go through the market, the contract notes will be marked PT
Receiver	(Administrative Receiver, as defined by the Insolvency Act 1985, s.45). An accountant (usually) appointed by a debenture holder in certain circumstances to protect his interest. Supersedes the directors' authority and normally involves an early suspension of the share price
Redemption yield	The running yield on a fixed interest security adjusted for average annual loss or gain on redemption
Retained earnings	Net profits after tax, dividend payments and adjustments for extraordinary items
Return on capital	Usually expressed as net profits *before* tax and depreciation as a percentage of net assets *before* depreciation. There are alternative definitions which result in quite different rates of return, using the same basic data
Rights issue	Where a company offers shares below current market price to existing ordinary shareholders in proportion to their existing holdings
Scrip issue	Bonus issue of fully paid shares to ordinary shareholders in proportion to their existing holdings
Senior debt	Secured loan in a leveraged buy out
Shadow option	This can arise on a refinancing where a company is in the hands of its bankers. The banker is offered a block of options with the exercise price falling as borrowing increases, to give the lender an additional interest in the firm's recovery

Short sale	Where stock is sold which is not owned, the seller anticipating falling prices will enable him to cover his sale lower down the market

Source and application of funds statement	A summary statement appearing as part of the annual report and accounts, typically:
	A. Source of funds
	  1) Retained earnings or profits
	  2) Cash received from asset sales
	  3) Proceeds of share and rights issues
	  4) Also technical adjustments in respect of items which do not involve actual movement of funds, e.g. depreciation and minority interest in retained earnings

Less	B. Application (expenditure) of funds
	  1) Dividend payments
	  2) ACT and mainstream corporation tax
	  3) Purchase of fixed assets
	$A - B = $ *net movement of funds* representing increases/decreases in cash, stock, debtors, creditors, i.e. working capital movements

Special situation	Any share where interesting and usually short-term developments are expected. Includes recovery stocks and deal stocks
Stag	Speculator who applies for shares in new issues anticipating a premium over the offer price, with a view to selling the letter of allotment at a profit
Swap	Long- or short-term debt or currency futures exchanges. Spot currency transactions simultaneously arranged with forward transactions
Technical position	Broadly, the amount of stock of a particular share in relation to the current demand for it. Technical influence on share prices is short-term, as opposed to fundamental influences which are concerned with basic factors underlying share value. Essentially the firm's trading prospects over the medium and longer term (see fundamentals)
Tender offer	Offer for sale where investors' bids for shares determine the striking price
Trade	Either a purchase or sale of shares. A purchase and sale is a bargain. Hence, statistically two trades equal one bargain
Transfer deed	A document transferring shares which is signed by the seller, returned to the stockbroker for settlement and registration
Warrant	Negotiable long-term option to buy shares at a fixed price. See also Bearer stock

Bibliography

Acres, W. Marston, *The Bank of England from Within*, 1931.
Alderman, G., *The Railway Interest*, 1973.
Allen, Trevor, *Ivar Kreuger*, 1934.
Beckman, Robert, *The Downwave*, 1983.
Berman, H. D., *The Stock Exchange*, 1963.
Birkenhead, 2nd Earl of, *FE (a life of F. E. Smith)*, 1965.
Boesky, Ivan, *Merger Mania*, 1986.
Boyle, Andrew, *Montagu Norman*, 1967.
Buchan, John, *Sir Walter Scott*, 1932.
Bull, George and Vice, Anthony, *Bid for Power*.
Carswell, Donald, *Sir Walter*, 1930.
Charlesworth and Cain, *Company Law*, 1983.
Clapham, Sir John, *Economic History of Modern Britain*, 1938.
  The Bank of England, 1966.
Clarke, Sir Edward, *Benjamin Disraeli*, 1926.
Cleaver, G. and P., *The Union Discount*, 1985.
Crick and Wadsworth, *One hundred years of Joint Stock Banking* (a history of the Midland Bank from 1836–1934), 1936.
Cunningham, William, *Growth of English Industry and Commerce*, 1929.
Dale, Ernest, *Long Range Planning*, 1969.
Davies, Hunter, *George Stephenson*, 1977.
Duff, David, *Albert and Victoria*, 1972.
Eames, John Douglas, *The MGM Story*, 1979.
  The Paramount Story, 1985.
Eiteman, Dice and Eiteman, *The Stock Market*, 1969.
Erleigh, Viscount, *The South Sea Bubble*, 1933.
Ford, Henry, *Today and Tomorrow*, 1926.
Galbraith, J. K., *The Great Crash*, 1954.
Gash, Norman, *Peel*, 1976.
Gilbart, J. W., *Theory and Practice of Banking*, 1873.
Giuseppi, John, *The Bank of England*, 1966.
Graham, Dodd & Cottle, *Security Analysis*, 1962.
Green, Timothy, *The New World of Gold*, 1982.
Greenwald, W. L, *Statistics for Economics*, 1963.
Greenwall, H. J., *Northcliffe*, 1957.
Griffith and Mayer, *The Movies*, 1972.
Groves, E. B., *Investing in the Stock Market*, 1987.
  Postcode Marketing Gazetteer of Great Britain, 1989.
Guedalla, Philip, *The Duke*, 1931.
Harrington, Michael, *The Other America*, 1971.

Hearnshaw, F. J. C. (ed.), *Prime Ministers of the Nineteenth Century*, 1926.
Hirschhorn, Clive, *The Warner Brothers Story*, 1980.
Hoyt, Edwin, P. Jnr, *The House of Morgan*, 1968.
Hyndman, H. M., *Commercial Crises of the Nineteenth Century*, 1892.
Jantsch, Erich, *Technological Forecasting in Perspective*, 1967.
Johnson, Paul, *Consolidated Goldfields*, 1987.
Kendall, M. G. (ed.), *Sources and Nature of the Statistics of the United Kingdom*, 1957.
Kerr, A. W., *History of Banking in Scotland*, 1926.
Kindleberger, C. P., *Manias, Panics and Crashes*, 1978.
Knowles, L. C. A., *Industrial and Commercial Revolutions in Great Britain in the Nineteenth Century*, 1941.
Lambert, R. S., *The Railway King (A Life of George Hudson)*, 1934.
Lockhart and Woodhouse, *Rhodes*, 1963.
Malcolm, Sir John, *Life of Lord Clive*, 1836.
Mantoux, Paul, *The Industrial Revolution in the Eighteenth Century*, 1927.
Marjoribanks, Edward, *The Life of Sir Edward Marshall Hall*, 1929.
Martin, Sir Theodore, *The Life of HRH The Prince Consort*, 1880.
Mayer, Martin, *Wall Street: The Inside Story of American Finance*, 1959.
Matthews and Tuke, *History of Barclays Bank* (to 1925), 1926.
McDonald, Sir J. G., *Rhodes – A Life*, 1927.
McLeod, H. D., *Theory and Practice of Banking*, 1883.
Megrah, Maurice, *Paget's Law of Banking*, 1961.
Mill, J. S., *Principles of Political Economy*, 1848.
Minney, R. J., *Clive*, 1935.
Moneypenny and Buckle, *Life of Disraeli*, 1920.
Owen, Frank, *Tempestuous Journey (A Life of David Lloyd George)*, 1954.
Parker, C. S. (ed.), *Sir Robert Peel*, 1899.
Pasley, F. D., *Al Capone*, 1966.
Peel, Lawrence, *A Sketch of the Life and Character of Sir Robert Peel*, 1860.
Ponsonby, Sir Frederick, *Recollections of Three Reigns*, 1951.
Raw, Charles, *Slater Walker*, 1978.
Rogers, Donald, *The Day the Market Crashed*, 1971.
Rouse, Clive, *The Old Towns of England*, 1936.
Lytton Strachey, G., *Queen Victoria*, 1921.
Swanson, Gloria, *Swanson on Swanson*, 1980.
Sykes, Ernest, *Banking and Currency*, 1918.
Thomson, Malcolm, *David Lloyd George*, 1947.
Tomlinson, W. W., *The North Eastern Railway*, 1914.
Williams, A. H., *No Name on the Door* (A Life of H. Gordon Selfridge), 1956.
Williams, F. S., *The Midland Railway*, 1888.
Winchester, Marquess of, *Statesmen Financiers and Felons*, 1936.
Windsor, Duke of, *A King's Story*, 1951.
Woodham-Smith, C., *Queen Victoria, Her Life and Times*, 1972.

Acts of Parliament, Official Publications and other sources

Bank Charter Act, 1844

Companies Acts, 1844, 1855, 1862, 1908, 1929, 1948, 1967, 1976, 1980, 1981, 1985, 1989
Railways Act, 1921
Insolvency Act, 1985
Financial Services Act, 1986
Censuses of Distribution, 1950, 1957, 1961, 1971
Annual Abstracts of Statistics
Financial Statistics
Inland Revenue Statistics
Municipal Year Books
Bradshaw's Railway Guide (April 1959)
ABC Railway Guide (July 1923)
Inwood's Tables of Interest and Mortality, 1961
Jordan's Company Secretarial Practice, 1982
Dictionary of National Biography

Index

Aberdeen housing boom 59
ACC 29, 105
Account current 116, 120, 122
Account trader/trading 44, 141
Accounting convention, etc. 100
Administrative receiver 10–11, 13, 147
Administrator 13, 14
ADR 21, 26–27, 141
Advance corporation tax (ACT) 50, 77, 141
AERIAL 23
AFBD (Association of Futures Brokers and Dealers) 32
AIBD 32
Alpha stock 22, 34
Amsterdam 5, 7
'Angels' 58
Anglian Water 49
Annual general meeting (AGM) 10, 12
Annual report and accounts 9–10
Antwerp 4–5
Arbitrage 'suspension grip' case 96
Arbitraged rate of exchange 108–109
Arbitrageurs, etc. 44, 108–112, 141
Argentine bonds, etc. 135–137
Arithmetic average 85–87
Articles of Association 10
ASDA 108
'A' shares 54, 105, 107
Assenting shareholder 102
Asset strip technique 101, 103
Associated British Foods (ABF) 102–103
At the money (market) option 114–115
Attributable net profit 141
Auditors 13
Automated trading system (ATS) 33, 119
Average cost of capital 141

Babson, Roger 93
Balance sheet 68, 142

Balfour, A. J. and Gerald 37
Baltic Exchange 7
Bank Charter Act 1844 8, 37, 136
Bank of England 5, 8, 130, 135–136
Banks, suspension of payment 130
Barclays Bank 19, 133
Bargains marked 86, 139
Baring Crisis 134–137
Barlow Clowes 2
Barnato, Barney 38
Barrymore, John 39
Baruch, Barney 38
Base rate 57, 127
Bass 26
Bear 3, 44, 90–91, 97, 124, 142
Bearer shares and stocks 35, 54, 76, 142
Beckman 110
'Bed and breakfast' 84, 142
Below the line item 142
Berisford 102–103, 109
Beta stock, factor 22, 34, 142
BIFFEX 32, 121
Big Bang 16–17, 24, 27, 30, 33, 70, 73, 119, 140
Black Thursday (24 October 1929) 138
Block trader 142
Blount, Sir John 129
Blue Arrow 58
Blue chip 142
Boesky, Ivan 110
Bond, Alan 107, 111
Boomtowns 58–60
Bottom up forecasting, see End use analysis
Bourse (Bourse de Valeurs, Paris) 130
Bowley, Prof. A. L. 85
Breakeven price (options) 116–117
Bretton Woods Agreement 6
Briefings 69
Brierley, Sir Ron 105–106
British American Tobacco (BAT) 46, 102, 111

152

British and Commonwealth 28
British South Africa Company 42
British Telecom 79, 115
Brokerage, *see* Commissions
Brokers, *see* Stockbrokers
Brontë sisters 132
BTR 102, 121
Bull 3, 44, 90–91, 97, 124, 143
Business cycle 139
Business development loan 11
Business Expansion Scheme (BES) 45, 124–127
Business risk, *see* Risks, etc.
Butterfly 118
Buy signal 91
Buying in shares 75–76

Cable and Wireless 117
Calendar spread 118
Call option 114, 117
Cantor, Eddie 38
Capital gains tax 49, 81, 84–85, 117, 126, 138, 140
Capitalization issues 68
Capital reconstruction 15
Capone, Al 39, 42
Carnegie, Andrew 36
Cash flow 53, 102, 142
Cash (stock) market 27, 115, 120
Castlereagh, Lord 5
Census of Distribution 106
Certificate of incorporation 9
Chaney, Lon 38
Chapter 11 (US bankruptcy laws) 13, 109–110
Chart analysis (Chartism), etc. 75, 93, 96, 142
Chinese wall 142
Churchill, Sir Winston 39
Churning 46, 48, 142
Cinema admissions (US) 61–62, 64
City of Glasgow Bank 2
'City Man' 2
Clive, Lord 37
Clore, Sir Charles 101
Coloroll 99, 108
Combination (spread option) 117
Commercial rate of exchange 57
Commissions 25, 27, 70

Common stocks (US) 137
Companies Acts 3, 9–10, 13, 15, 34, 76, 103, 134, 136
Company formation 9
Company limited by guarantee 9
Company promoters 41, 126, 129
Company reconstruction 15
Company registration agent 9
Company reports and accounts 68
Company secretary 10, 12, 19, 68
Compulsory liquidation 14
Computerized settlement system, *see* TALISMAN
Computerized share register 19, 21
Concert party 143
Conditional acceptance 102
Connaught Latham 28
Connells 49
Consolidated Goldfields 42
Consols 55–56
Contract note 16, 70–72, 83, 116
Convertible loan stock 54–55, 102, 111, 121, 143
Cooper, Gary 38
Corporate raider 109, 111
Corporation Tax 76, 111
Coupon rate 143
Cover 48, 74, 143
Crashes
  1825 6, 8, 130, 133
  1839 6, 8
  1847 6, 8, 133
  1857 6, 134
  1866 6, 134–135
  1929 (Wall St) 38, 93, 122, 133, 137–138
  1974 7, 133
  1987 103, 133
Creditors voluntary liquidation 14
Cromer, Earl of 137
Cross-holding 42, 107
Currency arbitrage 108
Currency option 118
Cycle, etc. 48, 75, 94, 96, 139

Darien Company 130
Database 17, 23, 66–67, 143
Datastream 23
Date of record 83

153

Dealing costs 24–25, 70, 73
Deal stock 143
De Beers 42
Debenhams 101, 109
Debentures 2–3, 9–10, 14–15, 54, 107, 144
Debt/equity ratio, *see* Gearing
Declining markets 61–62, 139–140
Deferred interest house plan 128
Deferred shares 54
Delta stock 22, 24, 34
Diagonal spread 118
Dickinson Robinson 112
Directors 10, 12, 68, 79
Disclosable share stake 102
Discounted cash flow (DCF) 143
Disraeli, Benjamin 37, 130–131
Divestment 143
Dividend yields 55, 69, 73, 80, 86–87, 101, 143
Dividends 12, 53–54, 57, 80, 132
Dixons 49
Double taxation relief 25
Dow Jones Index 86, 137, 139
Doxford, M. L. 28
Dual capacity trading 17, 143
Dual exchange rate 57
Dun & Bradstreet 68

Earnings dilution 76
Earnings per share (EPS) 73–74, 76, 97–98, 140
Earnings yield 68, 86–87, 101
Eastern Counties Railway 132
East India Company 8, 30, 37
Economic theories 4, 34–35, 97
'Economic man' 1
Edelman, Asher 105
Edison, Thomas 64
Edward VII 131–132
Electricity privatization 80–82
Electronic market 24, 30, 35
Electronic price quotation, *see* SEAQ
Electronic settlement service, *see* TAURUS
Elwes Committee 22
End-use analysis 89
Enterprise zone 65, 126

Entrepreneur 119, 124, 126, 132
EQE Index 118
Equilibrium 97, 124
Equity 143
Equity derivatives 88, 115, 118
Ethical investor 45
Euro Index option 115
Eurocurrency bonds 143
European Options Exchange 118
Eurotunnel 49, 63–65, 72, 121
Ex all 143
Ex div 26, 83, 143
Ex rights 77, 143
Ex scrip (ex capitalization) 76, 144
Exchange fluctuations 123
Executive investor 45
Exercise price 114, 116–118
EXTEL services 21, 67–69
Extraordinary general meeting/ resolution 12

Fairbanks, Douglas, Snr 39
Federal Reserve banks (US) 6
FIMBRA 29, 32
Financial index numbers 85–86, 145
Financial instruments 4, 8, 119
Financial Ombudsman 144
Financial rate of exchange 57
Financial Reporting Council (FRC) 32
Financial Services Act 1986 28
FINSTAT 23
Fisher, Professor Irving 38, 93, 137
Fixed charge 11, 54, 144
Fixed interest bond (stock) 54–55, 86
Floating charge 11, 13, 54, 144
Floor trading 35
Florida land boom 59, 137
Forecasts, etc. 64, 88–91
Foreclosure 10, 128
FOREX 21
Forward sale, etc. 120, 123
Franchise 126, 144
Frankfurt 7, 22
Fraser, Sir Hugh 101
Fraudulent investments 127–128
Freeport 65

FT-Actuaries Index **69, 74, 87, 97**
FT-SE 100 Contract **115**
FT-SE 100 Index **27, 33, 75, 85, 87–88, 93, 95, 103, 115, 118, 119**
FT-SE Eurotrack Indexes **88**
FT-30 Index **74, 86–87, 100–101, 139–140**
Fund managers **140**
Fundamentals, etc. **3, 27, 48, 90–91, 97–98, 102, 124, 145**
Futures, financial and commodity, etc. **3, 8, 27, 33, 48, 119–121**

Gable, Clark **62**
Galbraith, Prof. J. K. **38**
Gamma stock **22, 34**
Gateway **108**
Gearing **99, 107, 115, 128, 145**
General Electric (GE) **110**
George I **129**
George II and George III **37**
George, David Lloyd **37, 41**
Geometric average **85–86**
Getty Oil **110**
Gilbert, John **38–39**
Gilt edged stock **30, 33, 55–57, 86–87, 145**
Glaxo **26**
Globe companies **40**
Goldsmith, Sir James **102**
Gold standard **6, 39**
Goodyear Tire **109**
Goschen, G. J. **136**
Greenmailer **38, 109**
Growth stock (yield) **48, 53, 73**
Guarantee, *see* Personal guarantee
Guaranteed income **127**
Guinness Insider scandal **28, 109–110**
Guinness Peat Group (GPG) **99, 105**

Hall, Sir Edward Marshall **40**
Hanson **26, 38, 70, 102–103, 105, 121**
Harris, Lord **41**
Hedging **123**
High risk investment **63, 114, 118**
High value added **61, 145**

Hill Samuel Registrars **19**
Holden, William **39**
Holmes à Court, Robert **105**
Hope, Bob **39**
House of Fraser **101, 109**
Hoylake **102, 111**
Hudson, Elizabeth **41, 133**
Hudson, George **131–134**
Hudson's Bay Company **30**
Humped yield **57**
Hunt, Bunker **37**
Hunt, Derek **108**

Icahn, Carl **109**
ICC (Sharewatch) **23**
ICI **26**
IEP **105**
IG Index **118–119**
Imperial Group **103, 109**
IMRO **32, 127**
Income tax/Inland Revenue **25, 66–67, 84–85, 101, 126–127**
Index betting **60, 118–119**
Index numbers, *see* Financial index numbers
Indexation **85**
Inflation **55–56**
Information networks **66–67**
Insider trading **38, 50, 110, 145**
Insolvency Act 1985 **10, 13**
Intellectual investor **45–46**
Interest rates, nominal, effective (APR) **56–57, 107, 127–128, 139**
International Petroleum Exchange (IPE) **32, 121**
International Stock Exchange (ISE) **7, 17–18, 22, 28, 30, 32, 34, 67, 128**
In the money options **114–116**
Intrinsic value **63, 114, 116–117**
Investment risks, *see* Risks
Investment time frame **3, 60**
Investment trust **145**
Investor compensation **29**
Investor profiles **43–49**
Investors **3, 24, 36, 60, 73, 79, 82, 91, 96–98, 99–100, 108, 117, 119, 127–129, 138–140**
Irregular fluctuations **74–75, 93**

155

Isaacs, Godfrey and Sir Rufus 37
ISC (Institutional shareholders committee) 29
Isosceles 108
ISRO 29, 32

Jaguar 109, 116, 123
Japan 7–8
Jobber (*see also* Market makers) 16–17
Joint guarantor 11
Joint stock company 8, 30, 130
Joint venture 42–43
Junk bonds 8, 107, 145

Kennedy, Joe and John F. 38
Keynes, Maynard 37
Khedive of Egypt 131
Kingfisher 49
Kohlberg, Kravis, Roberts (KKR) 110
Kreuger, Ivar 40, 133
Kreuger and Toll 40

Ladbroke 105
LASMO 49, 70–71, 73, 87
LAUTRO 32
Law, John 130
LCE (London Commodity Exchange) 32
LDE (London Derivatives Exchange) 32
Leigh, Vivien 62
Letter of allotment 77
Letter of indemnity 19–20
Level playing field demand 145
Leveraged bids, buy outs, etc. (LBOs) 102, 107–108, 110–111, 147
Licence fees (FIMBRA members) 29
Lidderdale, W. 136
LIFFE 21, 30, 32, 33, 119
Limited liability; companies 8–12, 53, 135
Liquidation, etc. 11–12, 14, 111
Lloyds Bank 19
Lloyds of London 2, 7, 28, 32
London (City) 5–8, 22, 26, 30
London Futures and Options Exchange (LFOX) 32–33, 119

London housing boom (1978–1988) 59–60
London International 46
London Metal Exchange (LME) 32, 121
London Options Clearing House (LOCH) 32–33, 116
London Traded Options Market (LTOM) 32–33, 115
Long-term investment 61
Lonrho 18, 24, 38, 49, 101–102, 106–107
Lowndes Queensway 99, 108

McCarthy's services 23, 69
Managed investment 61
Management buy outs (MBOs), etc. 107–108, 145
Management ratio 102
Manweb 80–81
Marathon Oil 110
Marconi scandal 37–38
Margin requirements 38, 121, 138
Marginal share price 91
Market capitalization 146
Market makers, etc. 16–17, 24, 27, 34, 140, 146
Market sentiment 90, 96, 98
Marketing 146
Marley 50
Matching trades/matched bargains 22, 146
Maxwell, Robert 106
Medium-term investment 60
Melbourne, Lord 134
Members voluntary liquidation 14
Memorandum of Association 9
Menjou, Adolphe 38
Merger 103
Mezzanine finance 107, 146
MFI 108
M & G 105
MGM 39, 58, 62
Michael, Ralph 105
Midland Bank 19
Midland Railway 132, 134
Mill, John Stuart 138
Minimum contract 116
Minority interest (*see also* non-assenting shareholder) 103, 146

156

Mississippi land development scheme   **130, 133**
Monopolies and Mergers Commission (MMC)   **49, 102, 106**
More, Kenneth   **105**
Morgan, J. P.   **36**
Moving annual total   **75**
Moving average   **74–75, 96**

NASDAQ   **21**
National debt   **129–130**
National Power   **82**
National Westminster Bank   **19**
Navarro, Ramon   **39**
Negative yield   **146**
Negotiable securities   **54**
Negri, Pola   **39**
Net asset value   **54, 68, 75**
Net dividend   **68, 73**
New issues   **79, 98**
Newton, Isaac   **129**
New York   **6–8, 26**
New York Stock Exchange (NYSE), *see* Wall Street
Non-assenting shareholder   **103–104**
Non-voting ordinary shares, *see* 'A' shares
Norcross   **24**
Northcliffe, Lord   **66**
Northumbrian Water   **79**
Norton Warburg   **28**
Notice of Meeting   **12**

Ocean Transport   **50**
Off-balance-sheet debt   **100**
Offshore tax haven   **111**
Offshore trusts   **85**
Offer document   **64, 146**
Official Receiver   **14**
Ombudsman, *see* Financial Ombudsman
Options (traditional)   **33, 116–117, 119, 146**
Ordinary resolution   **12**
Ordinary shares, *see* Shares
Outhwaite Syndicate   **2**
Out of the money options   **117**
Over the counter market (OTC)   **24**

Overbought market   **124**
Overend Gurney   **134–136**
Oversold market   **124**

Pac-man defence   **111**
Paperless settlement   **19**
Paris   **5, 7, 22**
Peel, Sir Robert, I and II   **37, 133–134**
PE Ratio (multiple)   **26, 74, 86, 97, 102, 138, 140, 146**
Pennzoil   **110**
Pension contribution holiday   **102**
PEP (Personal Equity Plan)   **45, 46**
Perfect market   **34**
Period data   **74, 85**
Personal guarantee   **11, 52**
Personal liability of directors   **10**
Pickens, T. Boon (Mesa Petroleum)   **109**
Pickford, Mary   **39**
Pitt, William   **37**
Placing   **146**
Point data   **74, 85**
Poison-pill defence   **111**
Poll, right to demand   **12**
Polly Peck   **28**
Powell Duffryn   **50**
Powergen   **82**
Preference shares   **12, 54–55**
Preferential creditor   **14**
Preferred ordinary shares   **54–55**
Premium (options)   **114, 116–117**
Present value   **97**
Prestel City Service   **3, 23**
Price and value compared   **97**
Prince Consort (Prince Albert)   **131–132**
Private company   **9**
Privatization issues   **79, 107**
Professional registrars   **19**
Professional investors, *see* Investors
Professional speculators, *see* Speculators
Profit and loss account   **146**
Programme trading   **27, 119, 139–140, 147**
Prospectus   **147**
Proxy   **12–13**
PTM contract levy   **27, 73**

Public company 9
Public sector debt repayment (PSDR) 57
Punters 3, 43–44, 48, 111, 147
Purchasing power of £1 55–56
Put option 114–115, 117
Put through 147

QUOTRON 21, 23

Railway share speculation 131–134
Rally 93–94, 96
Random fluctuations, *see* Irregular fluctuations
Raskob, John J. 90
Rates of taxation 84–85
Rationalization 103
Ravensbourne Securities 19
Racapitalization 103
Receiver, *see* Administrative receiver
Receivership 13
Recession, definition of 98
Recovery situation 99, 105
Redemption yield 57, 147
Regis Registrars 19
Register of charges 10
Register of directors and secretary 10
Registered office 9
Registered shares 10, 18, 35
Registrar of Companies 9, 15
Regulated company 8, 30
Rentes 5
Residual seasonal 74
Resistance level 46, 91
Retail Price Index 55–56, 86
Retained earnings 147
Return on capital 1, 46, 147
Revelstoke, Lord 135–137
Rhodes, Cecil 41–42
Rights issues 77–79, 96–97, 115, 138, 147
Risks, etc. 1, 3, 51–53
RJR Nabisco 110
Robinson, Edward G. 39
Robinson, Sir Joseph 41
Rockefeller, John D. 36, 41–42, 133

Rowland, R. W. 107
Rothschilds 40, 131, 136–137
Rotterdam 7

SAEF 17
Sales index 39
Savings and investment contrasted 2
Savoy Hotels 107
Screen trading, *see* Electronic market
Scott, Randolph 39, 49
Scott, Sir Walter 130
Scrip dividend 26, 50, 76–78
Scrip issue 19, 76, 132, 147
SEAQ 17, 21, 23
Search fees (companies) 12
Sears 101
Seasonal fluctuations 74–75
Sector indexes 86–87
Securities and Exchange Act 1934 (US) 121
Securities and Investment Board (SIB) 29, 31–32, 61
Self Regulatory Organizations (SROs) 29, 32
Selfridge, H. Gordon 40
Selznick, David O. 62–63
Senior (secured debt), *see* Debentures
SEPON 17
Settlement 17–18, 44
SFA (Securities and Futures Authority) 32
Shadow option 147
Shakeout 93–95
Share arbitrage transaction 110–111
Share registration 10, 19, 26
Share warrants (bearer), *see* Bearer shares and stocks
Shares 2–3, 8–9, 12, 18–19, 34, 54–55, 76, 100, 107–108, 112–113
Sharif, Omar 40
'Shell company' 14
Sherman Anti-Trust Law 1890 (US) 36
Short sales 91, 123–124, 148
Short term investment 60
'Showstoppers' 111